Bantustan Gaza

Richard Locke
and
Antony Stewart

Bantustan Gaza

Richard Locke

and

Antony Stewart

Zed Books Ltd

CAABU

Council for the Advancement of Arab-British Understanding

*R005*42 92138

Bantustan Gaza was first published by
Zed Books Ltd.,
57 Caledonian Road, London N1 9BU and CAABU,
The Arab British Centre, 21 Collingham Road,
London
SW5 0NU in 1985.

Copyright © Richard Locke and Antony Stewart
1985

Typeset by Kate Macpherson Typesetting
Cover design and maps by Editpride
Printed by Cox and Wyman Ltd.

British Library Cataloguing in Publication Data

Locke, Richard
  Bantustan Gaza.
  1. Gaza strip — History
  I. Title   II. Stewart, Antony
  953'1   DS110.G3

ISBN 0-86232-582-X
ISBN 0-86232-583-8 Pbk

US Distributor
Biblio Distribution Center, 81 Adams Drive,
Totowa,
New Jersey, 07512.

Contents

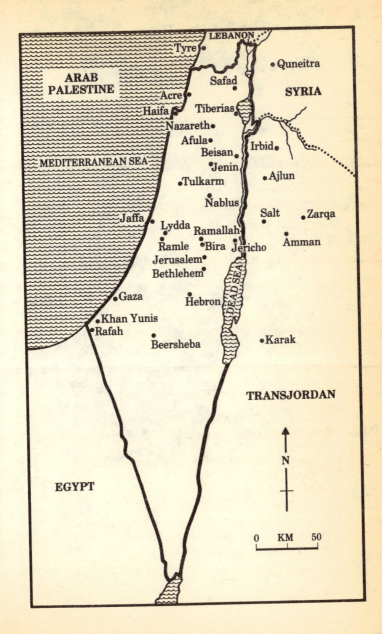

John Tordai

Making the desert bloom. A Palestinian farm on the edge of the Mediterranean in the south of the Strip. The Israelis want the land for a Riviera hotel complex.

This publication is dedicated to the many in occupied Gaza whom the authors cannot thank by name for all too obvious reasons, but without whose help it could not possibly have been written.

Richard Locke
Antony Stewart
June 1985

Foreword

by David Watkins
Director of CAABU

This appropriately entitled publication is the second in the current CAABU series. CAABU is publishing it jointly with Zed Press, whose resources and expertise will facilitate its introduction to a wider international readership.

The Gaza Strip is a crucial part of illegally occupied Palestine. Yet, although a great deal has been said and written about the West Bank, much less attention has been focused on the even more repressive regime inflicted upon the people in Gaza.

Nearly half a million people are crowded into that narrow strip of the Mediterranean coast. Three-quarters of them are refugees and descendants of refugees driven from their original homeland by the forcible establishment of Israel. Systematically deprived of the most basic human rights, they are concentrated into one of the most densely-populated places in the world.

In international moves for peace in the Middle East, there is a dangerous tendency to under-rate the importance of Gaza. But a peace which depends on treating Gaza as if it can be ignored or considered apart from the West Bank can never be achieved. The Palestinians of Gaza have as crucial a role in the peace process as their fellow citizens in the West Bank.

What follows is an historical and factual, rather than polemic, account of the nature of the Israeli occupation and of the importance of Gaza. But it is more than that, for the authors have lived in Gaza and what they have written is drawn from personal witness.

Introduction

So often journalists and academics either omit the Gaza Strip when discussing the Occupied Territories or tag it lamely on to the West Bank. For foreigners, particularly, who are perhaps used to strolling around Bethlehem or Jerusalem, the Gaza Strip is a daunting prospect. The climate is hotter and more humid; its people are poorer, its living conditions more crowded and oppressive. Overall it appears an unsophisticated and unattractive place which even few West Bankers visit. And while the West Bank has a number of legal, academic and economic groups with offices which can provide researchers with information, the Strip has only six personalities (a doctor, a lawyer, a former mayor, an UNRWA official and two women activists) who are prepared and able to meet journalists on a regular basis. All six live in Gaza Town. Typically, foreign visitors to Palestine squeeze a one-day visit to Gaza into the end of their trip and meet a couple of these personalities.

We were able to spend a longer period in the Gaza Strip and build up a wide range of personal contacts who showed enormous hospitality and warmth. This gave us a sense of what Gazans feel is important, which we hope is reflected in our work. The issue most discussed is the economic situation — rising prices and falling wages; this is followed by the politics, and in particular the current divisions within the Palestine Liberation Organization. During a recent visit to Gaza in February 1985 we found that very few people were optimistic that Yasser Arafat's growing links with King Hussein would lead to a just solution to the problem.

While no one doubts the legitimacy of the PLO as the sole representative of the Palestinian people, there is much criticism of the line being adopted by the current leadership.

Compounding Gaza's sense of isolation from the outside world is the belief that the Israeli occupation of Gaza is more repressive and more thorough than that in the West Bank. Gaza has no elected leadership, a higher percentage of its workforce labours in Israel, it has fewer nationalist institutions and its university, unlike those in the West Bank, has been unable to provide a community-based nationalist rallying point. Gaza is effectively a Bantustan — a dormitory for day labourers in the Israeli economy. It is for this reason that the much vaunted 'two state solution' has rather less appeal to the people of Gaza than to some on the West Bank.

The following is an introduction to Gaza. It looks at the historical experience of the Gaza Strip under three foreign powers: the repression of the British, the containment of the Egyptians, and the total incorporation by the Israeli occupation. It looks at how the Israelis have achieved this by military and then political means, opening their borders to Gazan workers, maintaining minimal education and health services while destroying local initiatives to improve them, imposing a legal system based on the British Emergency Regulations of the 1940s, emasculating UNRWA, thinning out the refugee camps through a policy of forced and voluntary resettlement, and finally by developing a network of Israeli settlements to control the scarce land and water resources and to create a Zionist presence throughout the Strip. It is a pessimistic account; but then it is difficult to find any real grounds for optimism other than the powerful determination on the part of every Gazan to stay put.

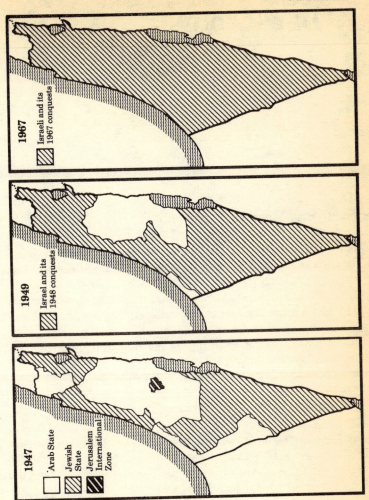

1967
Israeli and its
1948 conquests

1949
Israel and its
1948 conquests

1947
Arab State
Jewish
State
Jerusalem
International
Zone

1947 Partition Plan, 1949 Armistice, 1967 War

1. Background

The British Mandate

The Gaza Strip did not exist as a territorial unit until 1948. Under the British Mandate, it was part of the Southern district. The population took little active part in the Palestinian struggle against the Zionist movement and the partisan rule of the British, though they responded sympathetically to events in Jaffa, Haifa and Jerusalem. Once the British relinquished their responsibility and open conflict broke out, refugees began flooding into the Strip from 1947 onwards.

Egyptian Rule

By the time the final armistice was signed in 1949, some 200,000 Palestinians had been driven southwards from their villages. From the Majdal, Asdud and Bir Saba[1] areas and from Jaffa they came on foot, whole villages at a time, leaving everything except a few blankets and the keys to their houses. Everyone expected to be back home within weeks. They crowded into the only territory still held by the Egyptian army, taking shelter in mosques, schools, caves and groves, anywhere which offered protection from the encroaching winter. The area which actually became the Gaza Strip was only 6–10 km wide and 45 km long, an artificial entity a third of the size proposed in the Partition Plan for the Southern area [see map on p. 9]. The indigenous community of 80,000 was in no position to absorb the vast influx, economically or otherwise.

The Egyptian army set up a military administration with control over all civil and security matters. Municipal and village councils were appointed but there was no elected representation. Popular committees sprang up to meet the desperate medical and welfare needs of the refugees, but King Farouk, wary of allowing any political leadership to emerge, dissolved them. The Mufti Haj Amin el Husseini had been allowed to form an All-Palestine Government in Gaza after 15 May 1948; but even this conservative leadership was transferred to Cairo for fear it might provoke further Israeli attacks and there it soon ceased to be effective.

Political groups, especially the Communists and the right-wing Muslim Brotherhood, did attempt to organize, but they were severely harassed. Nasser imprisoned several Communists in the Sinai, some of whom, ironically, were later released and given political asylum by the Israelis when they invaded in 1956.

As it became clear that the Israelis were not going to let people return to their villages, eight refugee camps were established in the early 1950s and the UN Relief and Works Agency (UNRWA) was set up to administer health care, education and relief services to the refugees.

Two issues in particular helped to unify and politicize the stunned and debilitated population. Firstly, the Egyptians confiscated any arms held by Palestinians in an attempt to prevent them from infiltrating into Israel. In fact, Fedayeen raids on Israeli targets were usually the uncoordinated work of individuals, and most infiltration was by people returning to their houses for possessions or trying to get to Jordan. Even so, the Israelis responded with fiercely punitive attacks. The raid on Bureij camp in August 1953 by Ariel Sharon's special Unit 101 resulted in at least fifty dead and many more wounded. The refugees rioted the next day demanding arms and condemning the Egyptians for failing to defend them, but the Egyptians only tightened their own security, making Palestinian infiltration more risky rather than preventing Israeli attacks. Fedayeen raids continued, however, and became better organized under the coordination of an Egyptian, Mustapha Hafez.

The second issue was Nasser's attempt to reduce the refugee population by resettling them in the Sinai desert, outside Palestine. The scheme was proposed in 1954, with UNRWA's approval, and immediately provoked huge demonstrations and protests in Gaza. It was a focal point for activists to organize around, and for the first time the Communists and Muslim Brotherhood worked together. Nasser was forced to drop the scheme, but he was still unwilling to arm the people.

On 28 February 1955, the Israelis attacked Gaza Town and killed 39 people. Ben Gurion, the Defence Minister, was urging the Cabinet to authorize a full scale invasion, contrary to Prime Minister Moshe Sharrett's more dovish inclinations. On 1 March, Gaza demonstrated again, demanding arms with which to face the Israelis. By May Nasser had relented slightly, permitting training bases in the Strip for the Fedayeen, and in September took the decisive step to rearm by signing a major arms deal with Czechoslovakia, despite his virulently anti-communist stance.

Ben Gurion became Prime Minister in November 1955 and under his leadership the Israelis began preparations for an invasion, awaiting a pretext. It came in July 1956 when Nasser nationalized the Suez Canal. This move was felt to jeopardize British and French interests in the area. In November 1956 Israel invaded Gaza, while British and French troops attacked the Canal Zone.

The Israeli occupation lasted until March 1957. The little-known massacres in Khan Yunis and Rafah characterize both the brutality and indiscipline of this Israeli rule. Witnesses claim that over five hundred men were dragged from their houses, lined up along the wall and shot in cold blood. As in Deir Yassin,[2] the purpose of the massacres was to terrify people into leaving. One shade of Zionist opinion has always included the Gaza Strip in Eretz Israel and wishes it free of non-Jewish people. Compelled by US pressure, the Israelis withdrew, but in the short period of occupation they had made considerable efforts to entrench themselves. This was only a rehearsal.

Their withdrawal was seen as a great victory marked by a week of demonstrations. The Egyptians were welcomed back, the people preferring them to a UN mandate, and a new atmosphere of trust and confidence prevailed. Nasser encouraged economic growth and made some concessions to the Palestinians over determining their own future. In 1957, for the first time, Palestinians were allowed on the executive council of the administration, and headed the Health, Education and Welfare departments. In 1961, three years after the lawyers had begun work on a constitution for the Gaza Strip, a National Union was elected. A legislative council was then formed, half elected from the National Union and half appointed from the Palestinian members of the executive. The council had powers to pass new laws and amend existing ones, but under the law of the British Mandate the governor-general could veto any legislation unless it was passed again at the next annual session. Nasser was responding to the mood of restlessness, but he relinquished very little effective power. He continued to keep tight control over the emergence of a political leadership, especially of the left. Every move he made towards giving the Palestinians some political independence was designed to placate and pacify rather than to lead towards genuine independence from Cairo.

In 1964 the Arab League decided upon the formation of the Palestine Liberation Organization (PLO)[3] and Gaza delegates were sent to attend the first Palestine National Congress (PNC) in Jerusalem, headed by Ahmed Shukairy, the acceptable face of Palestinian nationalism. Nasser was thus relieved of sole responsibility for the Palestinians, having forced Syria and Jordan to participate. Offices of the PLO were opened in the Strip and people increasingly looked to it as a genuine nationalist leadership. The Legislative Council held its last session in 1966, but even before this it had been eclipsed and faded into the background.

The Palestine Liberation Army (PLA)[4] trained in the Strip, but guerilla groups were banned. Political organization was still subject to harassment by the Egyptians and only the Nasserite Arab National Movement was allowed any existence. The border with Israel was under the guardianship of UNEF (United Nations Expeditionary Force) and was at relative peace for a decade.

The Six-Day War

On 5 June 1967, Israel attacked PLA units entrenched in Khan Yunis, and the following night Gaza Town fell. A ceasefire was declared on 10 June, and Gaza found itself again under Israeli occupation. The most immediate tangible effect of the new occupation was the forced exodus of people. In May 1967 an estimated 385,000 people lived in the Strip. By the end of 1968, there were 325,000. Some 60,000 had either fled or been driven over the border into Jordan to become refugees for the second time.[5] The road and railway to Cairo were severed and Gaza became a part of the Israeli empire.

Notes

1. Now the Israeli towns of Ashquelon, Ashdod and Beer Sheba.
2. A village just to the west of Jerusalem whose population was massacred in 1948.
3. It was not until 1968 that the PLO came to assume its present structure and independent status.
4. The PLA is the military wing of the PLO as a whole and unconnected with the various guerilla groups.
5. Janet Abu Lughod, 'The Demographic Consequences of the Occupation', quoted in *The Gaza Strip: Heading Toward a Dead End*, Part 1, by Ann Mosely Lesch, UFSI Reports, 1984, No. 10, p. 6.

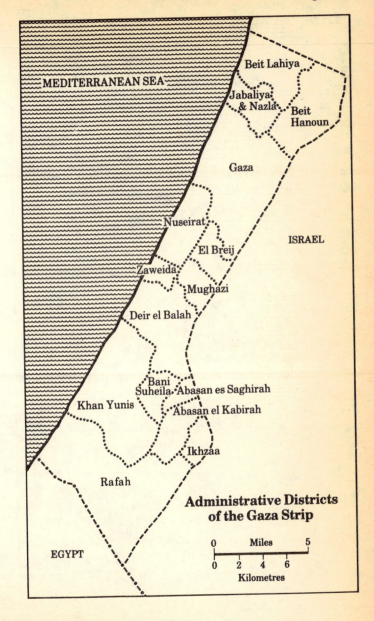

MEDITERRANEAN SEA

Beit Lahiya

Jabaliya & Nazla

Beit Hanoun

Gaza

ISRAEL

Nuseirat

El Breij

Zaweida

Mughazi

Deir el Balah

Bani Suheila

Abasan es Saghirah

Khan Yunis

Abasan el Kabirah

Ikhzaa

Rafah

Administrative Districts of the Gaza Strip

0	Miles	5

0	2	4	6

Kilometres

EGYPT

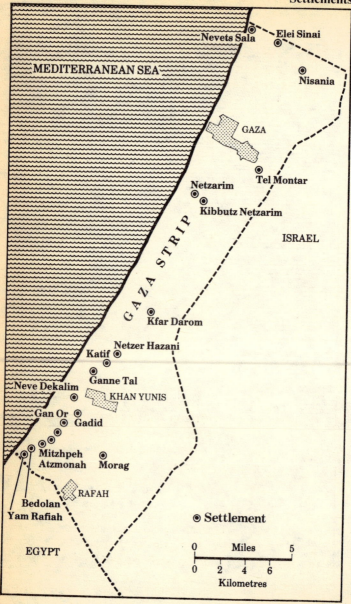

Settlements

MEDITERRANEAN SEA

Nevets Sala

Elei Sinai

Nisania

GAZA

Tel Montar

Netzarim

Kibbutz Netzarim

ISRAEL

GAZA STRIP

Kfar Darom

Netzer Hazani

Katif

Ganne Tal

Neve Dekalim

KHAN YUNIS

Gan Or

Gadid

Mitzhpeh
Atzmonah

Morag

RAFAH

Bedolan

Yam Rafiah

EGYPT

◉ Settlement

Miles

0   5

Kilometres

0   2   6

10

2. Gaza Under Israeli Occupation — Politics and Administration

Military Resistance

Military resistance to the occupation was initiated by the remnants of the PLA shortly after the June 1967 invasion. Aided by substantial quantities of arms left by the fleeing Egyptian forces, they were soon joined by other resistance groups, notably Fatah and the Popular Front for the Liberation of Palestine. The majority of the Fedayeen came from the refugee camps, where their familiarity with the maze of narrow passageways gave them an advantage over Israeli troops. For a period they were able to launch daily attacks on Israeli civil and military targets, but as time went on it became clear to most Gazans that the armed struggle had little chance of success. The geography of the Strip did not favour guerilla warfare, and the full potential of the Fedayeen was never realized because of the inability of the different military factions to coordinate their activities or develop complementary political organizations.

The Israeli response to the military resistance was systematic and ruthless. In 1971, under the direction of Defence Minister Moshe Dayan and Chief of Staff Ariel Sharon, the Israelis stepped up the repression in an attempt to crush resistance in Gaza once and for all. Student demonstrators were shot; 12,000 people, relatives of suspected activists, were detained in concentration camps in the Sinai and thousands more were deported to Jordan.[1] The refugee camps, the bases of the Fedayeen, were singled out for special treatment. Week-long curfews were imposed while

Sharon's troops conducted house-to-house searches. During these searches the male population of the camps were rounded up in market places or forced to stand waist deep in the sea for hours at a time. In July the army began levelling sections of the camps to allow easy access for armoured vehicles and to restrict the movement of the Fedayeen. Scores of Palestinian fighters were killed in the ensuing gun battles and by the end of the year the backbone of the resistance had been crushed.

The Gaza Municipality

Shortly after they occupied the Strip, the Israelis decided to place Gaza's electricity supply in the hands of an Israeli company. The mayor, Rajeeb al Alami, who had been appointed by the Egyptians, refused to sanction the takeover and was summarily dismissed from office. For the next three years the municipality was in the hands of an Israeli from the Interior Department. During this period the municipal services declined, so supporters of Rashad al Shawwa, a pro-Jordanian landowner, petitioned the Israelis to appoint him as mayor. The authorities agreed because it looked better to the outside world to have a Gazan at the head of the municipality. Shawwa was also recognized to have close links with Jordan. Having been left out in the cold under Nasser, he was now keen to stamp his mark on Gaza's future. Shawwa's appointment was by no means popular with all Gazans. While accepting the general principle that a local man should run local affairs, many people felt that unless headed by an elected official, the municipality could not become a forum for resistance to occupation and should be boycotted.

Shawwa made efforts to revive the economy and unsuccessfully attempted to secure an amnesty for the Fedayeen; but it was only a matter of time before he came into confrontation with the Israelis. In 1972 he was asked to extend municipal services to Beach Camp on the outskirts of the city. He refused on the grounds that this would compromise the refugee status of the camp and as a result was dismissed from office.

The Israelis were not able to find a local personality willing to take his place but they continued to seek ways of imposing a local government structure which might win the approval of the international community but would not compromise their own political or military objectives by creating a genuine leadership. They sponsored committees of conservative figures in the towns and camps from which a general council was to be elected. On the eve of the elections the leader of the Beach Camp committee was assassinated and the following day Shawwa was also the victim of an assassination attempt. Six of the eight committees resigned and the elections were cancelled.

In 1975 Shawwa allowed himself to be reinstated as mayor, but he inherited empty coffers. The municipality turned to the PLO for support which it received in return for the recognition of the PLO as the sole legitimate representative of the Palestinian people. Gazans responded by paying their taxes and the municipal officials, accompanied by PLO officials, were able to raise twelve million dollars from a rund-raising trip to Saudi and the Gulf.² The Israelis disliked the municipality's declaration of support for the PLO but were quite happy to see outside money being used, instead of their own, to maintain services in the Strip.

Many people in Gaza, however, especially on the left, were angered by seeing PLO money absolving the Israelis of their responsibilities. They also argued that because all decisions made in the municipality had to be approved by the military governor, the Israelis were able to channel outside money into the pockets of Israeli contractors.

Camp David

Anwar Sadat's 1977 visit to Israel was met with unanimous condemnation on the West Bank, but a small number of Gazans supported his visit. Shawwa and other conservative figures met with Sadat, and Sheikh Khuzundar, a prominent right-wing Islamic figure, led a delegation to Cairo in December. But it soon became clear to most of them that Begin's interpretation of autonomy, as outlined at Camp David, was unacceptable. Israel would retain control over land and water, the military government would remain, there would be a Palestinian council which would only administer, not determine, policy, and internal security (always a broad concept) would be in Israel's hands.

In October 1978 Shawwa held a public rally in Gaza, attended by members of the municipal and village councils, the professional associations, charitable societies and chambers of commerce. A declaration was issued by the participants of this Gaza National Conference, which was to be the last political expression allowed by the Israelis. The declaration is moderate in tone, stating the minimum claims of all Gazans. What follows is a shortened version of the declaration:

> 1. The Camp David agreement ignores the legitimate rights of the Palestinian Arab people, their right to freedom and self-determination and their right to create an independent national state in their homeland. The agreement also violates the United Nations Charter, the Declaration of the Rights of Man and the provisions of international law . . .
>
> 4. The agreement entrenches Israeli occupation for an unlimited period of time, endows it with legality, disrupts the unity of the Palestinian people at home and abroad . . . (and) does not specify the removal of the settlements in the West Bank and Gaza Strip . . .
>
> 6. A just solution to the Palestinian question can only be achieved when the rights of the Palestinian Arab people to their soil and homeland and to the exercise of their natural right to freedom, justice and self-determination are respected and when the Israeli forces have completely and immediately withdrawn from all occupied Arab territories.
>
> 7. The participants affirm that the PLO is the sole and legitimate representative of the Palestinian Arab people and that its participation on an equal footing with all other sides is essential for the achievement of a just solution to the Palestinian question. The cause of peace in the Middle East is not served by deliberately ignoring the PLO . . .

9. . . . The participants affirm that they fully support a just peace. They assert that the Palestinian Arab people aspire to that just peace. Of all the nations in the world, they need and desire this most in order to be rid of their sufferings and of the cruel fate imposed upon them against their will. They affirm that they have always been the victim of continuous wars and have been denied their natural right to freedom and a life of dignity on their own soil and in their homeland.

It is interesting to note first the reaction of Palestinians to a 'peace' settlement which was presented in the West as a triumph — Jimmy Carter's finest hour — and, second, the fact that seven years after that declaration was made in Gaza, Palestinians are still making the same requests, and still being ignored.

Following the declaration, a few conservative figures continued to make overtures to Sadat; but the mass of opinion was firmly opposed to Camp David. Sheikh Khuzundar led a second delegation to Cairo, but he was assassinated on 1 June 1979.

The military government responded by banning all political activities. Dr Heider Abdel Shafi, a leading nationalist figure, chair of the Palestine Red Crescent Society (PRCS) in Gaza, was placed under Strip arrest and the funds of the Red Crescent Society were frozen. The other associations faced similar restrictions.

Societies

When the municipality was taken over by the Israelis in 1972, the professional societies of doctors, lawyers and engineers moved to fill the vacuum of political leadership. These societies are really only social clubs and do not have the power to regulate even their own professions; but in the absence of alternatives, their leadership came to be seen as the Gazan leadership, although dominated by the traditionally powerful non-refugee families. At the forefront was the Gaza branch of the Palestine Red Crescent Society (PRCS), the Palestinian equivalent of the Red Cross. The PRCS ran a series of nationalist cultural events in the late 1970s which were enthusiastically received; it also ran literacy classes and provided health education talks and health provisions through its clinics. Following the near-total success of the leftist bloc in the 1979 elections to the PRCS executive, the Israelis, Gazan rightists and the Muslim Brotherhood set about its destruction. The conflict came to a climax in 1980 when a mob marched from the Islamic University to the PRCS and set fire to the building, unhindered by the authorities. Following this attack, new regulations were imposed which have effectively paralyzed all the societies. The PRCS is now restricted to running its clinics, and the other professional societies offer no real leadership.

Civil Administration

Israel's most provocative moves towards the Occupied Territories came in November 1981. First, alongside the military government, a civil administration was created to have responsibility for all non-security functions. Palestinians viewed the move as a manoeuvre to hide a military occupation behind a veneer of local autonomy and rejected it out of hand. The municipality went on strike after the civil administration was created, and in March 1982 the West Bank mayors were dismissed for refusing to meet the civil administration. The West Bank and Gaza erupted in the most violent demonstrations for years. For two months life in the Gaza Strip was disrupted. Seven people were shot dead in demonstrations and long curfews were imposed. On 4 May, Shawwa suspended municipal services and two months later he was removed from office. In August the other councillors were dismissed and the Strip reverted to direct military rule.

Second, the Israelis imposed a special excise tax on pharmacists and private medical practitioners. Tax inspectors raided medical clinics, confiscated accounts records and arrested two dentists. On 26 November 1981 the Arab Medical Association went on strike. They were soon joined by lawyers and engineers who feared that the same tax would be imposed on them. The strike spread to Khan Yunis and Rafah. Defence Minister Sharon ordered that the doors of 170 shops and 18 pharmacies be welded shut and striking merchants and professionals were fined or imprisoned. On 16 December, Shawwa ended the strike after negotiations had won a postponement of the tax.

Conclusion

Politically, a kind of stalemate exists in Gaza. The people have consistently refused to accept any settlement which might compromise their demand for a just solution to their cause, or their support for the PLO. However, Gazans have few channels through which to express their opposition to occupation. Political life under the Egyptians was either repressed or subordinated to a total faith in Nasser's promise of deliverance. The nationalist organizations which did develop after 1967, like the Red Crescent, were suppressed as soon as they were perceived as a threat. The Israelis have never allowed elections in Gaza, unlike the West Bank. After 18 years of occupation Gaza still suffers from the absence of a strong local leadership and popular organizations.

All Gazans put their hope in the PLO, but this hope is becoming increasingly ambivalent. The PLO has successfully put the Palestine problem on the world agenda, but the PLO speaks with many voices and its divisions have very negative consequences in Gaza. In particular, there is concern that money from the outside leadership is being used to buy and reward political supporters in the Occupied Territories, and that it is difficult to make political initiatives in Gaza without approval from outside. This situation has often resulted in political paralysis. There is a growing feeling in Gaza and among Palestinians living under Israeli occupation elsewhere that the relationship between the outside leadership and the Palestinians inside should be redefined to allow the latter a greater say in forging a strategy for opposition to Zionism. In May and June 1985, the Palestinian resistance in the refugee camps around Beirut was again beseiged, as it has so often been. These latest events are perhaps a tragic reminder of the necessity to find a way to build a resistance movement from within the Occupied Territories.

Notes

1. *Middle East Newsletter*, June–July 1971.
2. Personal interview with a former member of the Municipal Council.

3. Economy

Pre-1948

Gaza's economy was primarily agrarian. Unlike in other parts of Palestine where the land was divided up into smallholdings, most peasants were tenants of the big landowning families. The Shawwa family is thought to have owned 100,000 *dunums*.[1] There were some smallholders who tenured land on the *miri* system. (The land was leased out by the state, but in practice tenants acquired ownership rights and their descendants could inherit it.)

Gaza is an excellent fruit growing area, especially for citrus, dates, grapes and water melons. Most farming, however, was on a subsistence level with a variety of seasonal crops and very little production for export. Due to the lack of natural raw materials, few industries developed, though Gaza was famous for its cotton-weaving, and there was a soap factory. Other handicrafts included pottery and rug-making.

The major asset of Gaza Town, with a population of 36,000, was its small port providing the main outlet for the grain-producing Hebron and Beersheva areas. The barley supplied the German beer industry, while the wheat was consumed locally. The citrus industry was not yet sufficiently developed for export. Fishing provided another source of income.

Khan Yunis was a busy market town for the Gaza tribes of Bedouin from the Negev. There were some 70,000 Bedouin but their number decreased as their economy, which primarily depended on the sale of horses and camels, declined with the advent of the car.[2]

The British did very little to develop the Gazan economy and many workers had already migrated before 1948 to the larger ports of Haifa and Jaffa, where they lived in shanty towns.

Under Egypt

The war of 1948 and subsequent population increase virtually wrecked this fragile economy. With the imposition of borders, farmland was lost to the east, the Bedouin lost their grazing areas, and the port was cut off from the grain-growing areas. Over half the land area of the Strip was unproductive sand-dunes. The groves provided some low-paid seasonal work for the refugees, but there were no opportunities for work in the declining port, or in fishing and commerce. Some service jobs were created by UNRWA and the Egyptian administration. The vast majority of dispossessed Fellaheen, however, remained destitute for years after their arrival. In 1952, about 2,000 skilled workers and teachers were admitted into Saudi Arabia to work. Since then, the drain of skilled and unskilled workers to the Gulf countries has continued. Families left in Gaza have survived off remittances from relatives working in the Gulf.

After the Israeli invasion of 1956, Nasser sought to inject some vigour into the Gazan economy. Egyptians imposed strict currency controls on remittances from the Gulf, so these were deposited in Beirut banks. Gazan merchants then went to Beirut and purchased wholesale luxury goods which they then sold in Gaza. The economy improved after Nasser made Gaza a tax-free port attracting Egyptian holidaymakers denied such goods in their own country. Smuggling became a significant industry in itself.

Nasser also secured markets in Eastern Europe for citrus and offered loans, technical assistance and reduced customs as incentives. The citrus boom began with the area under cultivation escalating from 6,000 to 70,000 *dunums*.[3] Gulf remittances were invested in orange groves. By the mid-60s at least half the workforce was employed by the citrus industry. The East European countries, short of hard currency, often paid in construction materials and machines.

Under the Israelis

The immediate consequence of the 1967 war was a drastic deterioration in employment. Service jobs with the Egyptian army and the UN Emergency Force[4] disappeared, trade, smuggling and tourism with Egypt came to an end, the port was closed, and the fishing and construction industries virtually collapsed.

In the first year of occupation unemployment increased to 13.3% of the male labour force.[5] With the combined GNP of Gaza and the West Bank only 2.6% of the Israeli GNP in 1967, Gaza was not able to resist the incorporation and absorption of its economy into Israel's. There were objections to this from Labour Zionists who wanted to retain the Jewish character of labour in Israel, and from those Israelis who feared the demographic consequences of effective annexation. Defence Minister Moshe Dayan, however, realized the twin advantages of expanding the Israeli market and drawing upon the vast army of reserve labour, without the necessity of formal annexation. His aim was to answer Israel's servicing and economic needs by encouraging Gaza's dependence on Israel. It was a two-edged sword: Gaza's resources of land, labour and water would increasingly come under Israeli control, while the shops and markets of Gaza would be filled with Israeli goods.

Migrant Labour

In Dayan's original conception, the number of Gazan workers in Israel would be strictly limited; but in every year till 1974 the number grew. Between 1968 and 1972 Israeli employment agencies were set up in Gaza,[5] though until the military resistance was crushed in 1972 the PLO tried actively to prevent Gazans commuting to work in Israel. Today, of a labour force of

Table 3.1
Gaza Strip: Population 1983/2000

	1983	2000
Northern Zone		
Gaza City	148,416	313,120
Gaza Beach Camp	32,000	—
Jabaliya/Nazla Town	14,912	90,192
Jabaliya Camp	35,000	—
Beit Lahiya	11,172	40,190
Beit Hanoun	9,067	30,380
Total Northern Zone	*250,567*	*473,882*
Central Zone		
Deir El-Balah	25,078	80,000
Nuseirat	22,434	36,120
Breij	13,045	23,570
Mughazi	9,231	10,310
Zawaida	2,458	4,440
Total Central Zone	*72,246*	*154,440*
Southern Zone		
Rafah — City	20,719	80,000
Rafah — Camp	38,000	—
Khan Yunis City	50,885	114,080
Khan Yunis Camp	22,700	—
B. Suhaila	8,854	16,000
Abasan Kbira	3,301	5,960
Abasan Sghira	6,034	10,900
Khzaah	2,849	5,150
Bayuk	2,667	4,820
Total Southern Zone	*156,009*	*236,910*
Grand total	*478,822*	*865,232*

Source: Israeli Government Statistics

about 83,000, at least 30,000 are registered workers inside Israel. They apply to an agency, undergo a security check and a work permit is stamped on to their ID card. The permit must be renewed every four months. Migrant workers are not permitted to join the Trades Union section of the Histadrut,[6] and although there is a branch of the Palestine Trades Union Federation in Gaza, no Palestinian union has ever been recognized by an Israeli employer and union activists face severe harassment. Registered workers pay the same social security contributions as Israeli workers although their wages are low by Israeli standards and the social services available in Gaza far inferior.

Alongside this regulated employment there is what some Israelis call the 'Arab slave market'. It is impossible to know how many people are working illegally in Israel, but Palestinians estimate that the number is about 40,000. A considerable number are under 17 and cannot work legally. Employers often prefer children and women because they are cheaper. These unregistered workers congregate near Gaza Town's central post office from dawn onwards. Some are selected by Israelis to work in gardens, on home improvements and other casual labour. During fruit and vegetable picking seasons, there are usually few men or boys left standing about by eight o'clock but in the off-season, those who have not been picked drift away to cafés and back home. Unemployment in Gaza is a new and growing phenomenon because of Israel's economic crisis. Figures are unavailable because there is no system of registration and those who cannot find work often go to help a friend or relative with housebuilding and so would not consider themselves unemployed.

For those who do find work in Israel, hours are long and pay is low. Someone from Rafah, for example, working in Tel Aviv, has to allow four hours travelling per day and often more when a punitive roadcheck is imposed at the entrance to Gaza, which can cause delays for several hours. Because of this, a sizeable percentage of Gazan labourers sleep at their workplace where by Israeli law they must be locked in from the outside as it is illegal for Palestinians from the occupied territories to sleep inside the Green Line. Apart from horrifying accidents where workers are burnt to death because they cannot get out of their 'dormitories', sleeping away from home has a harsh effect on family life. Workers who leave early on Sunday morning with a basket of sandwiches and cigarettes will not see their family until the next Friday night.

Israeli statistics between 1970 and 1980 reflect a shift in the composition of Palestinian labour in Israel which suggests more stable employment in factories and restaurants.[7]

Table 3.2
Gazan Employment in Israel by Sector

	1970	1980
Construction	47.4	44.2
Agriculture	40.7	18.1
Industry	8.5	21.1
Services	3.4	16.6

Based on *Statistical Abstract of Israel* figures.

However, construction and agricultural jobs tend to be taken by illegal day labourers for whom there is no security.

Agriculture

Before 1967, agriculture accounted for about a quarter of the employment in Gaza, particularly seasonal work in the citrus groves. Production was labour-intensive and most unmechanized. Now Israel has restructured Gaza's agriculture to Israeli requirements. Farmers are prevented from exporting to Israel products which might compete with Israeli agriculture. Since 1967, melons, grapes, olives, almonds and onions have all declined in output, according to local researchers. Farmers have been required to get a permit before planting *any* new vegetables or trees since 1983, with the result that the Israelis control the development of Gaza's agriculture, particularly in citrus.

Citrus

The rapid expansion of citrus in the 1960s has created structural problems in the 1980s. Citrus accounts for a third of the area under cultivation and 70% of agricultural exports. The Israeli ban on new trees and the cancellation of all development loans has left the industry to decline. The number of new trees planted peaked in 1975 at about 210,000 tons yield. By 1980, 2,000 *dunums* of old trees had to be uprooted never to be replaced, whilst other trees' yields decreased, resulting in a drop in production to 172,100 tons in 1980.[8] As the trees age, the size and quality of the yield deteriorate.

After 1967 the East European market was cut back as those countries declined to trade with Israel. Direct export to the West is forbidden as it would threaten Israel's markets. Citrus either goes to Jordan and on to the Arab countries, with whom Israel cannot trade anyway, or to Israel to make up any shortages in their domestic supply and to make juice and marmalade at prices which the Israelis dictate. Administrative fees must be paid to the municipality and the Israeli Ministry of Agriculture for export to Jordan. Taxation, border tariffs and currency exchanges erode any profit a merchant makes. One merchant said that it was impossible to actually break even given the costs of maintaining the groves properly. Merchants and farmers view the squeeze on citrus as a deliberate policy to take labour off the land.

In December 1984 the Jordanian authorities struck another blow at Gaza's citrus industry with their announcement that Jordan would no longer buy Gaza fruit. Jordan previously purchased about 10% of Gaza's crop. Now the Jordanians are concerned to sell their own crop. However, 50% of Gaza's citrus will still be exported through Jordan to the Gulf states.

The Federation of Citrus Producers in the Gaza Strip, headed by Hashim Atta Shawwa, wrote to the Jordanian Minister of Agriculture asking him to remove the restrictions. Shawwa also criticized the Jordanian demand that farmers should only use boxes manufactured by Arabs for the export of citrus. According to Shawwa the only existing Arab box factory is incapable of supplying enough boxes, and more importantly, Gazan farmers have a trade agreement with Yugoslavia which obliges them to use boxes imported from Yugoslavia as payment for citrus. Between 25 and 40% of Gaza's crop is exported in this way. The dual problems of marketing and maintaining the groves have forced many farmers to abandon citrus production. At present there are 50,000 *dunums* of citrus, a third less than in previous years.

Israeli marketing companies have encouraged production of specialist items such as aubergines, courgettes and strawberries. The village of Beit Hanoun, to the north of Gaza, now has a large strawberry cooperative. The growers are, however, totally dependent on Israel to market the strawberries. If they do not want them they are left with rotting crops and no loss support grants. At the same time, Gazan farmers have to compete with subsidized Israeli produce on sale in Gaza. Indeed, marketing is the key and the Israelis control it, as they control price, quantity for export and even which produce should be grown.

Water

Control over and access to water means independence and power and this the Israelis have set about seizing. The lack of natural catchment areas in the Strip was compensated for by the existence of a water table underlying the Strip, rich in sweet water. Since 1967 there has been no free water; counters have been placed on the farmers' own wells and water has been rationed. Overpumping by Israeli farmers has become a serious problem with the intrusion of sea water into the aquifer and the consequent deterioration in the quality of the citrus and the drinkability of the water. Israeli experts concluded that pumping needed to be reduced by 30–60% to prevent terminable salinity. There is a ban on new wells, but this applies only to Palestinians; to the east and in the Strip itself, Israelis are sinking new wells deeper than those of the Gazans to supply the famers across the Green Line and the agricultural needs of the settlements. The disruption of Gaza's natural aquifers will rob Gaza of a crucial natural asset.

Manufacturing Industry[9]

Craft industries were always a traditional part of the Gazan economy, second in importance to agriculture. Production was mainly geared to the home market. Raw materials were imported and products passed through a number of workshops to the finished product.

Under the Egyptians, the natural growth of craft industries was stunted by the steady increase in the imports of finished products and consumer goods as merchants tried to evade Egypt's currency controls.

Table 3.3
Imports in Gaza (tons)

Year	1953	1954	1955	1959	1960
Raw	283	262	170	90	60
Finished	10	26	160	230	290

It is not clear from the statistics what form the finished products took, but the result was that a lot of people went out of business. In 1953, 2,500 people were employed in cotton-weaving alone, with 2,000 looms. By 1958, the total number of people employed in craft industries, including cotton-weaving, was 1,782 and there were only 50 looms.

The nature of craft industries has altered. What production there was, was geared away from the home market, with cheap labour being used for finishing products. The cottage industry was destroyed. Few capitalists wanted to invest in industry because the political situation was so unstable, and the Egyptians discouraged large factories for fear they would become the targets of Israeli air-raids. Only citrus was actively encouraged by the Egyptian authorities and it rapidly became the biggest employer and virtually the only investment.

Under the Israelis most people began to seek work in Israel where potential wages were higher. Craft industries slowly adapted, importing Israeli equipment and becoming more efficient. There is still an absence of industry proper in Gaza, but somewhat surprisingly it would appear that crafts are on the increase again. This is partly a reflection of the fact that the wages offered in Israel are no longer much higher than in Gaza when travel expenses are deducted, and the fact that people prefer to work from home for less. Industry remains a fraction of the total GNP but is increasing, as the following table illustrates.

Table 3.4
Per cent of total GNP of the Gaza Strip

Year	1968	1973	1975	1977
Industry	3.5	4.4	6.4	7.7
Agriculture	28.1	19.8	20.5	22.9
Construction	4.2	9.7	12.4	11.5
Trade/Transport/Service	62.5	35.5	30.6	29.1
Workers in Israel	1.7	30.6	30.1	28.9

The problems of Gazan agriculture similarly beset craft industries. Most workshops claim to be working at half their potential capacity because of problems of marketing and heavy taxation. But since 1979 the number of workers has been increasing in local industry, particularly in paper, plastics and other non-metal production. Industrial income has increased fourfold in real terms between 1970 and 1976. There is clearly room for growth, though at present industry is still a marginal activity in no way offsetting the predominant trend of Gaza's economic role as Israel's bantustan.

The following table indicates the kinds of crafts in which Gazans are occupied. It should be noted that most workshops are only working at about half their potential.

Table 3.5
Industry in Gaza

	No. of workshops	No. of workers
Sewing	11	150
Finishing clothes	81	644
Rugs	37	770
Furniture	27	112
Building materials	84	428
Metal work	41	331
Technical metal work	33	123
Pottery	16	39
Leather work	9	30
Grinding	9	18
Olive presses	3	9
Sesame presses	3	8
Bakers	13	48
Printers	9	35
Tea packers	5	26
Ice makers	3	13
Sweet makers	6	42
Ice cream makers	2	19
Glass dyers	2	12
Rice packers	1	8
Cosmetic makers	1	20
Plastics	3	60
Fat makers	1	25
Pesticides and pharmaceuticals	1	6

Trade

Gaza's growing reliance on the Israeli economy is revealed in Gaza's trade figures.

Table 3.6
Gaza's Trade

	Other Foreign	*Jordan*	*Israel*
Exports to			
1968	54%	18%	28%
1973	31%	11%	58%
1978	7%	26%	67%
Imports from			
1968	27%	1%	72%
1973	9%	—	91%
1978	9%	—	91%

Source: Statistical Abstract of Israel, 1977.

The figures show clearly how the Israelis have eliminated alternative markets for Gaza within ten years. The vast majority of Gazan import merchants go through Israeli agents. Their biggest complaint, however, is taxation. Most merchants did not in the past keep very systematic accounts. The Israelis have exploited this by using their own system. If tax payments are late merchants have to pay fines plus interest. In addition, they are required to pay a deposit for next year's tax based on the previous year's payment. If this is late, interest must also be paid on the deposit! The tax system has ensured that few, if any, merchants in Gaza are getting rich.

Israeli banks control the banking system. The Bank of Palestine, re-opened in 1981 after a High Court appeal, cannot deal with foreign currencies or expand its capital. As such it is little more than a place to cash cheques in shekels. The bank filed an appeal in the Israeli High Court three years ago to allow it to deal with foreign currencies and to open other branches. On 23 February 1985, Hashem Shawwa, chairperson of the Bank of Palestine, received assurances from the Israeli Prime Minister, Peres, Defence Minister Rabin and the Bank of Israel that the Bank's request to deal with foreign currency would be attended to soon. Shawwa considers it the latest in a series of delays. Originally, the Israeli authorities objected to the bank's name, preferring the bank to be called 'Renaissance', which is the name of Geula Cohen's extremist right-wing Tehiya party. However, the Israelis' real objections are that the bank could become a viable source of investment. At present the black market, officially banned all over Israel and the occupied territories, is the way everyone tries to beat Israeli inflation. Just behind the gold market in Gaza Town the money-changers gather every day on the street. The bigger money-changers even have shops, and the black market is a thriving business for them; for the street dealers it is a livelihood. On occasions the Israelis attempt to clamp down but the dealing simply goes underground into shops and houses, only to fully resurface a few days later when the panic has subsided. Street money-changers are just as common a sight outside banks in Israeli towns. People normally convert a week's wages in shekels into dollars and then buy shekels in small amounts as they need them. Everybody carries at least two, often three, currencies with them. The black market will be a permanent feature of the economy whilst there is still inflation at 300–400%.

Conclusion

The skilfully created and now almost total dependence that Gaza has on Israel for work and goods has reached the stage where Gaza is effectively annexed, as Dayan had envisaged, without representation or political rights for Palestinians. The dependence may now be quite mutual as without the water, cheap labour and captive markets of Gaza, Israel's shaky economy may not survive. This has obvious political implications for those Israelis and Palestinians who suggest that a two-state solution is a viable answer to the overall conflict, and points to a cruder and more repressive occupation in Gaza during recessions when Israel's demand for Palestinian labour falls off.

Notes

1. David Gilmour, *The Dispossessed*, London 1980, p. 23.
2. Ibid., p. 33.
3. Personal interview.
4. Metzger, Orth, Sterzing, Gottingen 1980, p. 88.
5. Ibid., p. 92.
6. Although often perceived as the equivalent of the TUC, the Histadrut is more than just a trade union. It functions as a para-state organization, owning a large number of companies, employing around a third of the Israeli workforce and providing extensive health and welfare services, almost exclusively to Israeli Jews.
7. Quoted in Ann Mosley Lesch, *The Gaza Strip: Heading for a Dead End*, Part 2, p. 7.
8. Ibid., p. 6.
9. All figures in this section, except where otherwise stated, from *Samed al-Iqtisadi*, Vol. 3, No. 19 (Arabic).

4. Education

The present 12-year educational system and the curriculum were established by the Egyptians. There are three levels: elementary (six years), preparatory (three years) and secondary (three years). The non-refugee population are not eligible for UNRWA education and must attend Israeli-run government schools. Refugees receive UNRWA education for the first nine years. Thereafter, they too must attend government schools. Half the population of the Gaza Strip is under 14, placing a heavy burden on the educational system. In 1982 the number of students was as follows:

Table 4.1
Numbers of students in Gaza

UNRWA	*Government*
Elem. 58,906 (girls 27,788; boys 31,118)	Elem. 38,000
Prep. 20,211 (girls 9,680; boys 10,531)	Prep. 10,000
	Sec. 18,000(inc. refugees)

Source: UNRWA and *Al Fajr* English, 1 October 1982.

School conditions may have improved greatly since the first years after 1948 when asphalt or sand served as blackboards and tents or barracks were used as classrooms; but they remain spartan. The average UNRWA school is a one or two-storey compound of breeze-block whitewashed classrooms with minimal facilities or equipment. The average class size is 45 and is often considerably exceeded.[1] Many pupils have to sit three to a two-person desk. No school has any heating or cooling system so in the winter classrooms are very cold and in summer stiflingly hot. Apart from a large blackboard, a teacher's desk and a chair, there is nothing else in the average classroom except rows of tightly packed bench-desks. Most schools have some wall posters, but there is little else to relieve the drab, functional atmosphere. With no sound-proofing or blackout facilities, noise and sunlight are constant distractions. Government schools look even less appealing. Like all the military installations, they resemble prisons with their nicotine-coloured walls and dark, guarded windows.

Teacher Training

The UNRWA education department, with the assistance of UNESCO, has built up a competent team of supervisors and teachers. Twenty years ago it was still possible to become a teacher with only the Tawjihi certificate (secondary school matriculation). Today all elementary school teachers must attend a two-year pre-service training course in Ramallah, in the West Bank, where they are trained to teach a full range of subjects and specialize in one subject. Preparatory school teachers must either be university graduates with one year's teacher training or must have had two years' training plus at least two years' teaching experience in their special subject. Since 1974, there has been an UNRWA Education Development Centre in Gaza which holds in-service training courses and provides enrichment material for the syllabus. Morale is generally high in UNRWA schools and teachers well motivated because of the monitored standards and reasonable salary.

It is extremely difficult to investigate government schools. Few teachers are willing to put their jobs at risk by speaking out, and foreign visitors are not welcomed by the Israelis. The teacher's salary is about three-fifths of an UNRWA teacher's, and some find they need a second job to meet their family's needs. The atmosphere of fear induced by political screening before being given a job and the careful watch kept on you thereafter make motivation very low. Government teachers receive practically no in-service training. Some request to be admitted on to UNRWA-held courses. As part of a deliberate policy, the Israeli Head of Education rarely grants permission to maintain the most minimal educational service. Schools inside Israel are infinitely better and the salaries of teachers three times higher.

The quality of education in government schools in Gaza is considered by academics to be inferior to education in the West Bank. West Bank and Jordanian students' marks are unofficially upgraded when set against Gaza Tawjihi marks.[2]

The Syllabus

The Egyptian curriculum is very long and difficult and largely irrelevant to the students' lives. It has been revised only to reflect the shifting political alliances in the Arab world rather than educational advances. Students are not encouraged to think critically but are expected to learn by heart vast quantities of facts. This pushes the teacher to adopt rote-learning methods. Since 1967 the curriculum has been under the scrutiny of the Israeli censor. Gazan students may be able to recite the names of the Egyptian pharoahs or the presidents of the USA, but are denied instruction in Palestinian history. Government teachers face very severe penalties if they attempt to bring Palestine into lessons. The curriculum thus fails to explain or directly contradicts the students' reality.

Israeli Interference

The education system was thrown into chaos immediately following the Israeli occupation in 1967. Many teachers either left Gaza during the war or were deported or imprisoned.

Schools soon became centres of resistance alongside the military struggle. Demonstrations were frequent until the early 1970s, especially in secondary schools. The army entered schools and hundreds of pupils were beaten and detained. One boy is now deaf, dumb and blind as a result of such a beating he received when he was eleven. The Israelis were keen to stabilize the situation quickly. The militant potential of crowded schools is a constant worry for them.

Under the rules of the Geneva Convention the Egyptian syllabus must be followed by all schools in Gaza. Despite this the Israeli authorities introduced Hebrew into government prep schools. UNRWA schools have successfully resisted this. All textbooks used in UNRWA schools coming from Egypt are censored, first by UNESCO and then by the Israelis. Books can be delayed for up to six months, by which time they may be out of print in Egypt. The shifting political alliances in the Arab world mean that textbooks are frequently revised to reflect such changes. The new edition of a book, even if it is identical, must again go to the censor. UNRWA's agreement with Egypt prevents it from accepting books altered by the censor. Thus, elementary and preparatory students are buying Israeli-produced expurgated copies in the Gaza markets rather than receiving them as UNRWA free texts. In the academic year 1983–4 only 35 out of 80 books were used in UNRWA elementary and preparatory schools because of the bans.[3] The education department has therefore to rely on costly workbooks they produce themselves. Arabic readers and almost all social studies books are banned, but even maths books are censored for the slightest reason. Certain chemicals are banned by the Israelis. As a result only 20% of experiments on the UNRWA curriculum are carried out.[4] This places science students at a serious disadvantage at the university level. Virtually no experiments are performed in government schools.

UNRWA schools are desperately overcrowded; but no new schools can be built due to the Israelis' refusal to grant building permits. In 1981, UNRWA wanted to build a school between Khan Yunis and Rafah because elementary pupils had to walk 8 km to school. The contractor, who had begun building on land

John Tordai

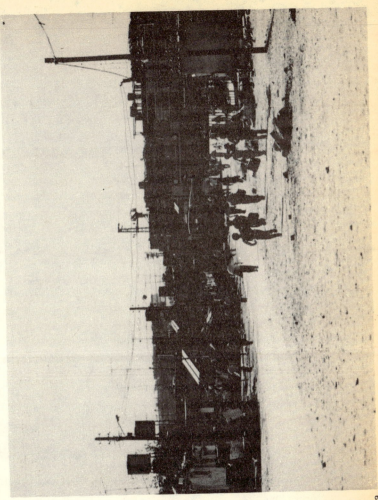

A main street in Gaza.

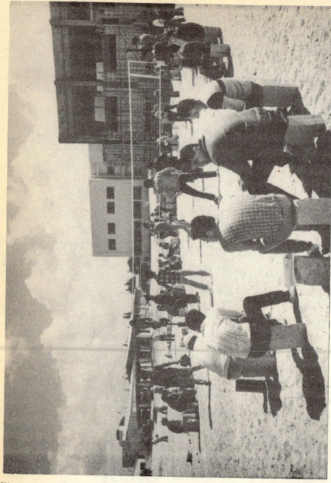

Paul Cossali

Islamic University of Gaza. More like a building site than a university. Students play volley-ball between lectures.

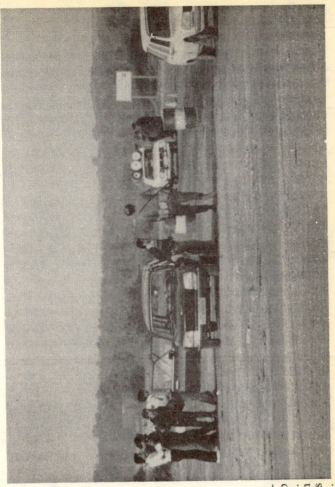

Paul Cossali

Eries Checkpoint. Palestinians returning to the Strip from Israel are searched. Since the bus-hijack in April 1984 the border has been rebuilt like a fortress.

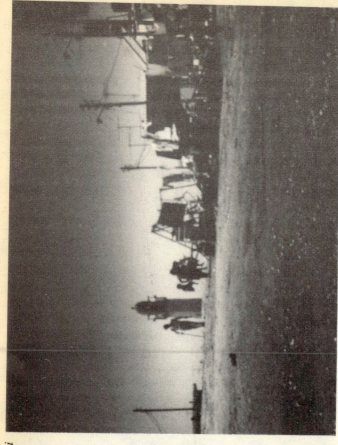

John Tordai

Thinning the camps. An area in Beach Camp cleared of homes to make way for Israeli tanks during Sharon's repression of military resistance in the early seventies.

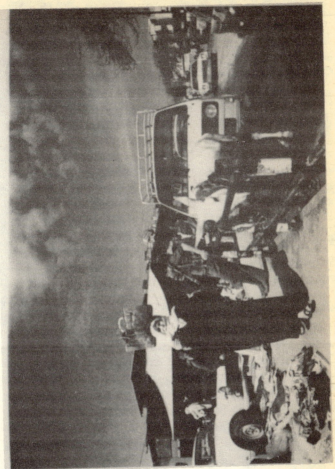

John Tordai

Gaza Town. Soldiers patrol the main market. Israelis come to Gaza to do their shopping.

Bureij Refugee Camp. Demolition of homes in Israel occupied Gaza
goes back to June 1967.
Kay Brennan/UNRWA

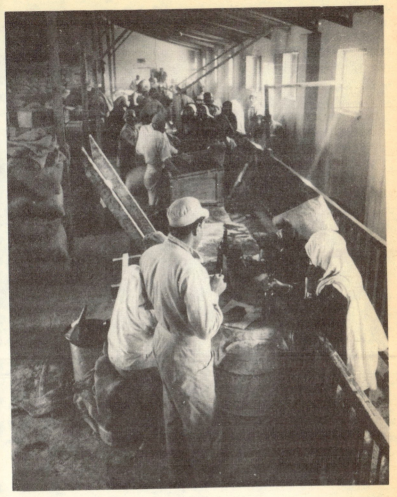

Distribution of UNRWA rations in Nuseirat camp.
UNRWA

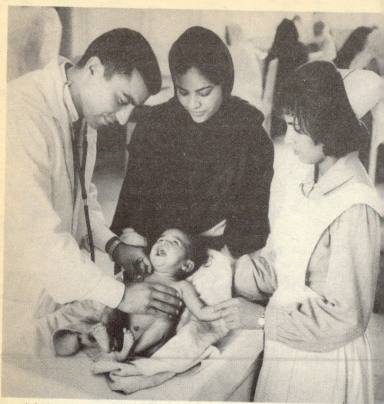

A baby about to be discharged from UNRWA's dehydration centre in Khan Younis camp. The centre was established with funds donated by the Canadian Save the Children Fund. Many children die from gastro-enteritis every year.
UNRWA

House demolition. A family in Beach camp living in a makeshift shelter. Their house was demolished by the Israelis because it was allegedly outside the Camp boundaries.
John Tordai

John Tordai

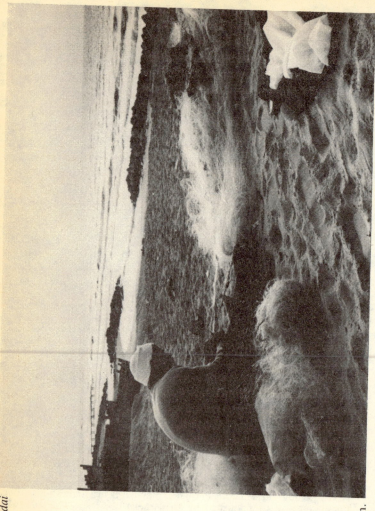

A Gaza fisherman.

donated by a local landlord with materials from an international agency, was arrested and building stopped.[5] Eighty-eight of the 105 elementary schools operate on a double shift with separate teaching and administrative staff. UNRWA is not allowed to take any more land for building schools and the construction of extra classrooms in the existing compounds is subject to permission. Last year the army entered an UNRWA school in Jabalia camp to prevent repairs to classrooms which were dangerous. The Israelis considered these repairs to constitute building without permission. At the time of writing the classrooms are now being repaired. The Israelis have built government schools close to the camps in an effort to discourage refugees from attending UNRWA schools. They would like to break down the refugee/non-refugee distinction, and by extending their control over education ensure that schools remain open, but not for learning.

After School

For the students who are successful in the Tawjihi there are few options. The Occupation authorities maintain five vocational training centres: two teacher training, two offering commerce studies and one agricultural studies. About 1,500 students are absorbed in these institutes. Until 1978 Egypt used to accept up to 1,500 students a year in its universities. Sadat closed the doors on the Palestinian students as a punishment for Palestinian hostility towards his peace effort. Delegations from Gaza to President Mubarek have so far won few concessions. This has been disastrous for Gaza's university hopefuls.

West Bank university places are scarce and competition fierce. The other option, to study in Europe or America, is beyond most families' financial resources and often involves learning another language for at least a year. Gaza now has its own university which currently enrols nearly 3,000 students.

Table 4.2
Gaza students enrolled in Egyptian universities 1969–1978

Subject	*No. of students*
Lawyers	741
Art faculties	852
Co-operative specialists	13
Doctors	494
Physiotherapists	39
Nursing	65
Dentists	87
Chemists	130
Engineers	483

(Most of the above will have graduated; only a few will be working in their chosen field.)

Source: A.S. Dahlan, Research Student, Durham University.

The Islamic University of Gaza

The Islamic University of Gaza (IUG) was founded in 1978, following the restrictions imposed on the number of Gazans allowed in Egyptian universities, allegedly because of Gaza's failure to welcome the Camp David accords. The IUG was built on the site of the Al Azhar religious institute with funds from Saudi Arabia, Jordan and the World Islamic Council, after a bitter dispute between the nationalist leadership, who wanted a secular science-based university on the lines of Bir Zeit University on the West bank, and the conservative religious elements. The Israelis were easily able to tip the balance and the building started. Even now, with its 3,000 students (38% of whom are women) and a hundred plus staff,[6] the university still resembles a building site. Facilities are limited and the campus is sex-segregated.

The IUG has become the base in Gaza of the Muslim Brotherhood. All students, irrespective of their discipline, must pass an initial year of religious studies which involves studying Islamic law and rote learning of sections of the Qu'ran. Much of the debate within the university centres on the extent to which non-Islamic subjects, such as education, should be taught within an Islamic framework. Some factions even want to see the English textbooks replaced by translations of Islamic works. Because of this, and because of the IUG's failure to involve itself in community projects such as literacy classes, the result has been disenchantment among progressive and nationalist elements, who look on it as a last-choice university. It has been rewarded by the Israelis with less interference than the West Bank universities, although in 1983 800,000 dollars of outside funding was frozen following the failure of the university to dismiss six lecturers in compliance with an Israeli-imposed work-permit system. Unless the narrow base of the university, as exemplified by its choice of trustees, is broadened, it will neither act as a focus for Palestinian national aspirations nor provide itself with a measure of protection from Israeli interference, nor even provide modern graduate education. In many ways, the problems of the IUG reflect the problems of Gaza itself.

In early 1985, a power struggle took place within the university between the religious elements and the secular nationalists. Two leading academics were shot dead and a bitter fight for dominance in the university ensued. It was said that Yasser Arafat was called upon to intervene and bring about an agreement following Abu Jihad's failure to do so. A power sharing agreement was worked out which was to guarantee an equal number of faculty deans from the Muslim Brotherhood and the centrist Fatah faction. This brought about a temporary lull in the in-fighting, but in April 1985 the Muslim Brotherhood attacked and hospitalized twenty nationalist students following the publication of a scurrilous pamphlet which made jibes at the religious leadership. It is alleged by staff at the university that this attack was organized by the university's administration itself and that they possess a list of 110 students and staff who are considered dangerous secular activists. This indicates the seriousness of the Brotherhood's intention to maintain their power base. It also indicates how the Israelis are able to profit from this in-fighting. The suggestion is that the Brotherhood's hostility towards the secular nationalists is so intense that they may, at times, have the same aims as the Israeli security forces. Indeed, those hospitalized by the Brotherhood were later arrested and taken from the hospital by the Israelis.

To an outsider, it is difficult to understand the seriousness of the political divisions within the university. In the absence of a political forum for Palestinians under the Israeli occupation to discuss issues freely, and given the protracted nature of the divisions within the Palestinian leadership outside, the struggle for dominance within the university takes on a sort of importance by proxy. Student elections, as with elections to the professional associations, provide a rare chance to express opinions on issues far beyond the brief of the organization itself. Likewise for the leadership outside, the elections provide some indication, however unreliable, of trends in public opinion. In Gaza's university, the fundamentalist bloc of students has always dominated the union. The results have typically been 70% fundamentalist, 25% Fatah, and 5% for the leftist alliance. This is not, however, a fair reflection of Gaza's overall political distribution. The fundamentalists, because of their access to funds and some acquiescence on the part of the Israelis, are over-represented. Conversely, most leftist students prefer to travel abroad or to the West Bank to study, which leaves them under-represented.

Future Trends

School students are not motivated to complete their studies, given the slim chance of a university place. This has resulted in a high percentage of drop-outs at the preparatory and secondary stages. The number of students that sit for the Tawjihi has not increased since 1967, despite the annual population growth of 3–4%. The number of drop-outs increased markedly after access to Egyptian universities was closed, but economic considerations also play a part. Some families need the extra earning power early on in a student's school career. Some boys under 16 are obliged to work in Israel and their future thereafter is permanently restricted to this insecure and arduous form of employment. Those with university places often have to give up before completing because they simply cannot afford to delay earning any longer. Graduates also fare very badly in the job market. Figures issued by the professional associations reveal that many engineers, doctors and lawyers are forced to look for labouring jobs in Tel Aviv because of the dearth of professional employment.

Table 4.3
Unemployment in professions in Gaza

Engineers Association 1984

Total registered	775
Unemployed	250
Working in Gaza	350

Lawyers Associations 1984

Total registered	256	
Articled	87	
Licensed	169	(68 work in their own office, of which only 40 cover their costs.)

Source: Figures compiled from information given to the authors by the professional associations.

The present economic recession in Israel hits Palestinian workers hardest, and the demand even for unskilled labour is now diminishing.

Education in Gaza is fast approaching something of a crisis. Despite UNRWA's potential to improve the quality of its teaching, it is still constrained by the compulsory Egyptian curriculum and Israel's control over all secondary education and educational planning. Any reforms UNRWA can introduce will only be in degree, not kind. Meanwhile, the up and coming generation of school children is larger than ever before, further straining an overburdened system. What seems to be emerging is a polarization between early school leavers who enter the diminishing Israeli job market with little education and few prospects, and a graduate class that is mostly under-employed. Expectations are still for university education, yet there are fewer and fewer chances, and a virtual absence of professional employment.

Opportunities in the Gulf, which has already absorbed vast numbers of professional Palestinians, may now be coming to an end as those countries' own education systems improve and their own citizens fill the posts formerly taken by Palestinians.

As Sarah Graham-Brown has noted, these high expectations reflect the Palestinian attitude to work and social status; but they are also the result of a lack in the education system of a middle ground. Charitable agencies attempt to bridge the gap, but do so only on a small scale. The Near East Council of Churches (NEEC) has secretarial and computer courses. UNRWA has its own Vocational Training Centre (VTC) and an American Baptist Mission runs a nursing school. Educators in Gaza have suffered from not being able to plan or structure education as they would like. They realize the need for more vocationally-oriented education, but cannot implement it themselves despite the acute needs Gaza has at this level of services.

Perhaps the most alarming development is the possible transfer of full control over education to the military authorities with the dismantling of UNRWA. This would definitely lead to a further drop in educational standards and leave the Palestinians no protection against cultural deprivation, disarmed in the one area where they still have some strength.

Notes

1. In 1985, new UNRWA regulations, precipitated by their cash crisis, have laid down that 200 teaching posts will not be replaced after retirement and that the minimum class size will be 50 students.
2. *Al Fajr* English, 1 October 1982.
3. UNRWA staff member (personal interview).
4. Ibid.
5. *Al Fajr* English, 1 October 1982.
6. Sarah Graham-Brown, *Education, Repression, Liberation: Palestinians*, London 1984, pp. 82–105.

5. Health Services in the Gaza Strip

Health services in Gaza can be divided into three administrative categories: UNRWA, government (i.e. Israeli), and privately-run services. UNRWA provides a basic and competent layer of curative medicine through its nine clinics (one in each camp, one in Gaza Town and two sub-clinics in outlying villages). But like all UNRWA services, shortage of funds and an increasing population place strains on their health provisions. They provide rehydration and nutrition facilities for babies, daily dental clinics in two of their centres and bi-weekly visits to each of their clinics by an ophthamologist. They have 126 beds in their maternity units where most women in the camps give birth. UNRWA doesn't have any hospital beds apart from a half share in Bureij Hospital, which is more of a sanatorium. However, they do pay 40% of hospital costs for registered refugees and 80% in special hardship cases.

The government runs 19 clinics, 14 of which are only open in the mornings. Three villages are without any clinic. They employ 60 doctors and 11 dentists in this network. Children under five receive free treatment. In addition, they run four hospitals and the other half share of Bureij Hospital. The biggest is Shifa Hospital in Gaza Town which has 336 beds and is currently being expanded. It has 60 doctors and 120 nurses. Nasser Hospital in Khan Yunis has 249 beds and it includes the Strip's only orthopaedic department with 25 beds. Thirdly, in Gaza Town, there is a pediatric hospital with 135 beds and a small ophthalmic hospital which also contains a 20-bed psychiatric ward. UNRWA does not provide specific facilities for the care of mental patients, though there is now a plan, initiated jointly with the privately-run Sun Day Care Centre in Gaza, to train a team of home-help psychologists and to build a special mental health unit in a UNRWA school. However, these ideas have still to be implemented.[1]

The Sun Day Care Centre is the only private institution catering for psychiatric needs. Its patients, who are given various forms of therapy and training in social skills, are mostly in the under-15 age group. The strains of living under occupation in an area also undergoing rapid social change have created severe mental health problems. The crisis centre at the hospital regularly deals with patients who become psychotic as a result of interrogation by the military authorities, or seeing others tortured.[2]

These services are supplemented by the Palestinian Red Crescent Society which runs five clinics and two dental clinics. Only a nominal charge is made and drugs are provided at just over cost price. The Near East Council of Churches runs three mother and child health centres in poor areas of Gaza Town. The Anglican Church runs a small but efficient hospital, although its cost puts it beyond the reach of many people. The Sisters of Nazareth, the Missionaries of Charity and the Pontifical Mission all run a small service which does not, however, make a major impact on the health of Gaza.[3]

This dry statistical run-down really says very little. Since 1967, the Israelis have manipulated the health services to create a dependency which strengthens their control. Provision of health is an integral arm of occupation and occupation involves destroying local initiative while trying to show in some way that the occupation is benevolent.

Infant mortality rate (IMR) is normally regarded as the best indicator of the state of health. UNRWA estimates that the IMR among Gaza's refugee population was 71 per 1,000 live births in 1973 and that this rose to 88 in 1980. Of these deaths, over half were caused by gastro-intestinal or pneumo-bronchitic diseases, both of which are considered preventable. Israel states that the IMR in Gaza is 41.3, yet studies on the West Bank have indicated that the IMR in the refugee camps tends to be lower than in outlying villages because of the lack of running water and other infrastructural deficiencies in the latter. Gaza's IMR is unlikely to fall while the camps run with open sewers and rats, the traditional diet is eroded by Israeli manufactured foods, and waste disposal services remain inefficient.

Government-run services are characterized by a shortage of funds, overcrowding (two people in a bed is not unheard of), understaffing, outdated equipment and a shortage of specialized facilities. Gaza has no qualified anaesthetist, heart, pediatric or chest surgeon and only one psychiatrist. (Israel has 2,000.) Yet there are 60 unemployed doctors in Gaza working as labourers in Israel and a host of specialists working abroad.

Independent initiatives to improve this situation have been stifled by the military authorities. The Red Crescent was refused permission to build a hospital which had been planned and funded; the reason given was that the Israelis felt that health services should be centrally organized, i.e. by the Israelis. Gazan doctors from the Arab Medical Association were refused permission to run a voluntary health education programme which involved visiting schools to give talks to students. A doctor in Jabalia who collected a team of volunteer doctors to hold a part-time clinic in the camp was threatened by the military. Yet Gaza has 1.5 beds per 1,000 population (Israel has 3.2) and one doctor to 1,500 patients (1 to 600 in Israel).

In the 1970s, the Israelis introduced a voluntary health insurance scheme. Everyone over 16 must pay about $8 per month, with some cheaper rates for families with many children. Patients who are not insured pay about $75 per night for a hospital stay. Probably a little over half of the population is insured. Only government employees and some workers in Israel are obliged to pay.

Ostensibly, the system aimed to establish a regular health budget to develop the health infrastructure, but this has not proved the case. The health budget between 1979–81 actually fell by an annual 8% in real terms. In addition, it is believed that a significant amount of the money collected in the Strip is not spent there.

The Israelis justify the shortage of specialized services by pointing to the referral system to Israeli hospitals of patients who cannot be treated in Gaza's hospitals. There are two problems here. Firstly, this referral system takes up 30% of Gaza's health budget — money which is paid to Israeli hospitals when Gaza has the specialist doctors but lacks the facilities. Secondly, it is alleged that there is a quota system which results in long delays and the unlikelihood of being referred in the last week of the month when the quota is usually complete. In some ways, health provision has actually deteriorated since 1967. During the Egyptian period, health care was free and patients requiring specialized care would be treated freely in Cairo. The key to any health system is planning and funding, and the Israelis control both very carefully. Health services cannot genuinely improve within the context of Israeli occupation.[4]

Notes

1. *Health Services in the Gaza Strip*. An Independent Survey, Bir Zeit University, 1983.
2. *Middle East* magazine, January 1985.
3. Planning for Health in Occupied Palestine, Rita Giacaman (undated).
4. 'Disturbing Distortions', a response to the report of the Ministry of Health of Israel to the 36th WHO Assembly on Health and Health Services in the Occupied Territories, Geneva, May 1983; and interviews with Gaza health workers.

6. Law [1]

The draconian laws enforced in Gaza by the Israelis are inherited from different sources: some from the British, some adapted from the Egyptian administration and some military orders created to plug the gaps. These orders do not have the status of laws, but one Palestinian lawyer estimated that they are used in 85% of military court cases. The British Defence Emergency Regulations of 1945, initially applied to prop up the struggling British Mandate, form the basis of the Israeli military law in the occupied territories. The British governor was given the authority to detain without trial, to demolish homes, to impose collective punishments, to deport activists, to impose curfews and declare areas closed for military purposes. Although these laws were condemned by Zionist jurists in 1945 as being comparable to the laws of Nazi Germany, the occupying authorities still make full use of them.

During the Egyptian period, these laws fell into disuse except in cases involving treason or spying. There was a gradual move towards a rather tepid autonomy from Cairo with a locally-elected legislative assembly assuming powers of local government and law enforcement.

This process was abruptly terminated in 1967 following the Israeli invasion of the West Bank and Gaza Strip. In addition to the rigid application and exploitation of the Emergency Regulations, the Israelis transferred areas of jurisdiction such as tax assessment and customs from the civil courts to the military courts. There has been a general deterioration in the quality and scope of the civil courts. Despite a significant population increase as well as an increasingly complex set of business directives to administer, there are actually fewer judges than before 1967. The civil courts are run like a business: the fines section has been expanded so that the courts realize a profit at the expense of providing an equitable system. One result of the lengthy delays in cases being heard is that the traditional system of solving disputes by the two families in contention sitting together with a respected intermediary, usually a mukhtar, has increased.

The scope of a 'security offence' is so broad that it includes possession of illegal magazines, posters, flags and maps, unlawful assembly of more than five people, failure to report an offence or planned offence against the occupation authorities, a traffic accident involving a military vehicle or any expression of support for an illegal organization. In July 1984 an artist from Jabalia camp was jailed for six months for incitement in one of his paintings being exhibited at the Islamic University in Gaza. The red, white, black and green of the Palestinian flag had been used. In addition, he was heavily fined.

Detainees can be held for 18 days by the Shinbeth (Israeli secret police) without a charge being brought. After 18 days the Shinbeth can seek a renewal of the detention from a judge who hears a statement from the Shinbeth and the suspect. Several renewals can be obtained. After 105 days the detainee must be brought to court or released. However, there is nothing to prevent a detainee being recalled shortly after release. A detainee is brought to court having signed a confession (in Hebrew — a language which many Gazans speak but do not read or write). Conviction can be made on the basis of the confession. This system encourages torture which the vast majority of prisoners claim they are subjected to in interrogation. There are various types of torture, but the most common are beatings, being kept awake and not fed for long periods, being subjected to degradation, cold showers and electric shocks. Being asked to collaborate is a standard practice, since most people need something from the authorities: permission to travel cross-border, building permission, jobs and money or trading licences. As well as sowing seeds of doubt in the community about known activists, the Israelis have also succeeded in building up an efficient network of collaborators. Many people recount stories of how their interrogators knew about intimate conversations they had had with trusted friends.

The powers of the prosecution in military cases have been further extended by a new amendment that allows for a suspect to be brought to trial and sentenced without a personal confession. A statement by someone else or a refusal by the suspect to confess is now sufficient for prosecution. Previously, if the Israelis wanted to detain someone beyond 105 days and had failed to obtain a confession they resorted to administrative detention. Under Article 38 of the British Emergency Regulations the Shinbeth could bypass the judge after 105 days and seek renewal of detention direct from the military governor. Abdullah Eish has been under administrative detention since 1979. He has been physically destroyed during his detention, and is now deaf and dumb and dependent for his life on a glucose drip. Now if the Shinbeth wish to have someone imprisoned, they can do so through the courts without obtaining a confession.

The result is that lawyers who work for the defence of detainees find themselves in a hopeless situation. For a confession to be deemed inadmissable, the onus is on the defence lawyer to prove that the defendant was tortured. This involves knowing who did it, and as most detainees are hooded during interrogation and as 18 days (or longer if needed) is long enough for physical evidence of torture to have disappeared, this defence is very rarely successful. Lawyers describe the military court as a theatre: the verdict has been scripted in advance. They view their only role as trying to reduce sentences. Some try to do this by insisting on the political rather than the criminal nature of the charges, some by adopting the opposite position that the suspect is just a criminal with no political motivation. Neither strategy seems very effective. Indeed, several lawyers in Gaza refuse to work in the military courts because they believe it is a waste of time and their presence only serves to provide a degree of legitimacy to the proceedings.

In prison, apart from bad food and sanitation and extreme overcrowding, most people cite the neglect of emergency health needs as the worst abuse. The majority of long-term prisoners suffer from haemorrhoids. A simple operation is denied prisoners, in one case for seven years, while they suffer internal bleeding. Ulcers and cancer are also common. There are at most two doctors attached to a prison. Recently allegations were made by a group of Palestinian lawyers that doctors and nurses are involved in assisting the Shinbeth to persuade prisoners to collaborate with them. The Israeli Medical Association has yet satisfactorily to deny these allegations.

The overall effect of the application and abuse of military law is a sense of paralysis among activists and would-be activists alike. Occupation is so total and so sophisticated that it smothers and suffocates. The professional guilds, for example of lawyers, doctors and engineers, have been curtailed by a recent ruling which states that the agenda for any meeting they want to hold must be submitted to the military authorities for inspection 40 days before the meeting is due to take place. Funds from outside the Strip are also forbidden, as are fund-raising activities in the Strip. To establish a new society, its aims must be submitted to the authorities for approval. The result is that the only societies which have been founded since 1967 are small-scale social service-type institutions such as an old people's welfare association and an orphanage.

In this respect, Gaza differs from the West Bank for historical reasons. Between 1948 and 1967, Gazans placed their hopes in Egypt and Abdel Nasser in particular to solve the Palestinian problem. Because of this trust, it was not felt necessary to establish the network of unions, women's groups and professional guilds that sprang up in the West Bank to channel opposition to the more conservative Hashemite regime. When the Israelis occupied Gaza in 1967, there was a minimal framework through which to oppose them. By stringently applying a set of laws which place few constraints on them, by carefully nurturing Gazans' dependence on Israel for their survival and by exploiting the power of fear on those who slip through the net, the Israelis have made organized opposition extremely difficult.

Notes

1. Based on interviews with three lawyers in Gaza, September 1984.

7. UNRWA [1]

Given Gaza's economic dependence on Israel and its repressive rule of law, UNRWA at first sight seems to offer the Palestinians their only buffer against occupation. The ubiquitous blue flags raised above UNRWA's 322 installations in the Gaza Strip are as much a part of the bird's eye view as the solar-heating panels on every roof. Yet to the refugees these flags are ambiguous symbols. Importantly they enshrine the refugee status of Palestinians in the face of the constant attempts of the Israelis to deny it. But for many Palestinians these flags represent a non-political paternalism which has sapped their nationalist struggle. What lies behind such allegations?

From the outset the United Nations appeared to recognize that the refugee problem would not be solved without the return of the refugees to their land. Resolution 194 stated that the refugees should be permitted to return to their homes, and compensation paid to those who chose not to return. Israel let no one return. In the face of such intransigence the UN capitulated, and instead sought to 'promote economic conditions conducive to the maintenance of peace and stability in the area'. UNRWA was thus established on 8 December 1949 and began operations six months later. The existing emergency relief programme, set up by the UN with the assistance of the Red Cross and the Quakers, was taken over by UNRWA. The aim was to rehabilitate the refugees over a five-year period. This strategy was no doubt motivated by a genuine desire to alleviate the squalid conditions of the refugees, but there was also a hint of something which to the Palestinians was more sinister. As the UN Economic Survey Mission commented, 'The opportunity to work will increase the practical alternatives available to refugees, and thereby encourage a more realistic view of the kind of future they want and the kind they can achieve.' The economic development of the host countries and the integration of the refugees within them was to be promoted as a basis for permanent resettlement: an infrastructural bandage for a political wound. UNRWA was intended gradually to fade into the background.

Nasser's scheme to resettle refugees in the Sinai was met with approval by UNRWA, but that scheme and the whole strategy of UNRWA during that period were soon recognized to be unworkable. The refugees strongly resisted any move which might have jeopardized their right to return. They refused any improvement to their living conditions which implied permanency even if it were to their immediate benefit. Even the planting of trees in the camps was resisted.

From this point on, the Agency gradually changed from a short-term emergency body to an organization with quasi-governmental responsibility. Its mandate came to be regularly renewed by the General Assembly, with no end to it in sight, and likewise no end to Israel's expansionism and obstruction of a just solution.

The Agency's operations are based upon two conflicting principles. Firstly, it cannot function in territory controlled by a state without that state's consent. Yet secondly, its mandate is to safeguard the interests of the Palestinian refugees. It has no territorial or legislative power and no jurisdiction, and yet it is required to provide relief provisions, education and health. With its powers so closely defined and restricted, UNRWA can neither bring about a political solution nor bestow upon the refugees more self-government than Israel will allow. Since 1967 Israel has persistently interfered in the Agency's operations and it has been powerless to do more than appeal against this.

The Camps

UNRWA provided the first camp shelters in the early 1950s. Each family received on average an 11m² room plus a bit of open space. Forty-eight thousand rooms were constructed in the eight camps. Agency photographs from that period give the impression of suburban housing estates, row upon row of neat little boxes; but the reality was somewhat different. People from the same village by and large stuck together so that even today the camps have a strong village identity, keeping alive through oral history the sense of belonging and desire to return. Over time the refugees have extended their shelters so that the camps have become mazes with narrow lanes. With assistance from UNRWA the refugees have built private latrines, and the last public bath house was closed in 1978. Most people now have running water in their shelters, taken from UNRWA wells, municipality connections, MEKOROT (Israeli Regional Water Supply Co.) and from private connections, legal or otherwise. The UNRWA water allowance is 20 litres per person per day. MEKOROT charges for all water except in hardship cases.

The sanitary conditions in the camps are appalling. Refuse collection does not keep pace with what is thrown away so that there are always piles of rubbish festering in the street. UNRWA has been providing materials for self-help projects to lay concrete paths and drains. At present there are only open sewers running through the camps. It would require financial resources beyond those of UNRWA to make other than cosmetic improvements to conditions in the camps. Plans by the Community Development Foundation (CDF), an American aid agency, to build sewers in the Rafah Camp in 1980, were rejected by the Israelis.

Services

UNRWA initially concentrated on providing relief services, which accounted for 80% of the budget; but these are now only about 26% of the budget. Most of the money used to go on monthly basic rations of flour, rice, sugar and oil. In recent years the rations have been supplied in kind by donor governments. In September 1982, after 32 years, the rations were suspended in order to divert funds to Lebanon. As a result 182,000 beneficiaries lost their rations. There are 20,000 hardship cases who have continued to receive rations.

Education is now UNRWA's main service, accounting for 57% of the budget. UNRWA has nine health centres providing comprehensive out-patient services, and six maternity wards, and trains nurses and midwives. There are supplementary feeding centres for the malnourished and health education in schools. Following a WHO survey, more emphasis is now being put on dental care. For serious medical cases UNRWA cannot provide treatment. Since 1967, 65% of the refugees have joined the Israeli health insurance scheme.

Administration

UNRWA is everywhere, whether it be the blue and white of the identical school buildings and uniforms, or the buses and cars that ply up and down the Strip despatching employees, patients and officials. People grumble about this or that service as they would of a government. Inside the headquarters there is an appearance of orderliness that the rest of Gaza lacks. The neatly trimmed lawns, swept asphalt and fresh paint seem like relics of bygone colonial administrations. Despite the fact that UNRWA provides work for 3,473 refugees and 257 indigenous Gazans, its control from outside has injected a certain complacency into the organization. The five international staff, and beyond them Vienna, run the show, while the Palestinians defer. This malaise is perpetuated by the emergence of a group of Palestinian officials who, by no longer living in the camps, are felt to have lost touch with camp life. UNRWA has spawned its own nouveau riche.

Future Prospects

UNRWA has long lived under the shadow of financial insolvency. Ninety-five per cent of the budget comes from the voluntary contributions of governments. The USA has always been by far the biggest donor, giving it, some would argue, effective control. Though it no longer pays the two-thirds of the budget it once did, it still pays a third. The other big donors are Europe and Japan and the EEC. Their contributions are in line with America's: if the USA withdrew support it is extremely likely they would follow suit. American support for UNRWA has always been controversial, and in recent years given on the condition that the money shall not be used 'to furnish assistance to any refugee who is receiving military training as a member of the so-called Palestine Liberation Army or any other guerilla-type organization, or who has engaged in any act of terrorism.'[2] Mrs Kirkpatrick, the US ambassador to the United Nations, has led a campaign against American support for UNRWA, arguing that although once a humanitarian organization, UNRWA is now political and a threat of Israel's, and *ipso facto* America's, interests in the region. Against this line of argument State Department officials maintain that UNRWA has been primarily responsible for the maintenance of stability in the region, and that it is definitely serving America's interests to keep it there. (An argument Palestinian leftists often use to decry UNRWA.) The issue has yet to be resolved, but America's contribution has diminished, forcing UNRWA to make cuts in services and to seek funding elsewhere.

Twenty-six million dollars was cut from the 1985 budget to offset the standing deficit of 67 million dollars. The revised budget of 165 million still exceeds the expected cash income of 138 million. On 11 January 1985 UNRWA's Commissioner-General Olof Rydbeck, announcing the budget cuts, promised 'the cuts will be made with the aim of not impairing UNRWA's education, health and relief services for Palestinian refugees in the Middle East.' The refugees in Gaza find this hard to believe. No new schools or clinics will be constructed, there will be a general freeze on the hiring of new staff, a decrease of up to 50%

in the budget for travel, transport, educational supplies and equipment, and building maintenance will be deferred.

The reaction of refugees to the suspension of rations has been, in some cases, desperate. In Jabalia camp only 13 hardship cases were added to those eligible for rations. With unemployment on the increase again some families are dependent on the rations. Many people feel that the suspension of the rations programme was just the beginning. The fear is that the refugees will be forced to depend more heavily on Israel for services, with dire consequences both in the quality of services, and the political control that would give Israel. It is easy to criticize UNRWA, yet it has ensured a quality of life which the refugees would otherwise have been without, and for better or worse its fate is now inextricably bound up with that of the refugees. The international community has always tended to regard the Palestinian problem as a refugee problem rather than a national problem. Without UNRWA, Israel may be able to claim that the refugee problem has been solved. They would of course be obliged to assume the responsibility for minimum services for the Strip, though it is likely America would provide finance for this. The issue of resettlement — moving refugees out of the camps — most clearly illustrates the dilemma of Palestinians and of UNRWA.

Notes

1. UNRWA's Public Information Office, Gaza. This office has a large number of pamphlets, reports and studies, as well as an excellent collection of photographs which are all available free on request. The information in this section was drawn from a variety of UNRWA sources.

2. Quoted in Milton Viorst, *UNRWA and Peace in the Middle East*, p. 2.

8. Resettlement

The visible reminder the eight refugee camps provide of the dispossession of 1948 constitutes a thorny problem for the Israelis. As focal points of Palestinian identity and militant resistance, the camps, as perceived by the Israelis, require constant army surveillance. Faced with this hostile and resentful population herded together, the Israelis have sought to break up their concentration, and in so doing to sever the refugees' link with their homeland and their desire to return to it. Yet in purely practical terms the rehousing of the refugees is an enormous task. The latest scheme was unveiled by Minister Ben Porat in November 1983, a refugee resettlement programme costing $1.5 million to rehouse 30,000 refugee families over a five-year period. Speaking at a press conference, Porat described the Israelis' intention to erase the camps as humanitarian and voluntary, but failed to indicate how his scheme might work in practice. American aid is to finance the programme, which fuels Palestinian suspicion that the programme is only a prelude to expulsion of a substantial percentage of the refugee population.

The initial idea of resettlement originated in 1971 when Ariel Sharon ploughed 50m wide roads through the camps to facilitate army patrols in his suppression of military resistance. The shelters of 2,554 families were destroyed, and only 395 of them were accommodated in vacant UNRWA shelters. Five hundred of these displaced families were shunted over the Egyptian border to Canada Camp (named after the Canadian contingent of UNEF who camped there after the October 1956 war). In

1982, after the Camp David Accords, these families were stranded on the Egyptian side, cut off from work and family and prevented from receiving full UNRWA services by Israeli border controls. Every day families shout news and endearments across the barbed wire as insouciant Israeli soldiers look on. Another 200 families were forcibly transferred to Tel as-Sultan housing project after their houses had been swept away for the 1982 border. The families in Canada Camp are still waiting to be rehoused in Tel as-Sultan. In all, 10,000 shelters have been destroyed in Israeli demolition schemes between 1967 and 1984.[1]

This systematic destruction of people's homes raises the question of who owns the camps. In December 1982 the Israeli authorities, without consulting UNRWA, issued an order making selling, buying, mortgaging, exchanging, transferring, building or adding to the camp shelters an offence. Penalties for violators were stated in the order:

> Whoever may act contrary to these orders will have to remove the buildings at their own expense, otherwise he will be subject to withdrawal of the said buildings from him, or will have to pay a fine in cash or will be imprisoned, or will have both penalties inflicted on him simultaneously besides and beyond the removal of the building at the expense of the contravenor.[2]

Unlike the Egyptian orders, which aimed to regulate the unplanned expansion of the camps, the Israeli orders are of a punitive and repressive nature within an overall political aim. Ownership and jurisdiction of the camps were never clearly laid down, but they were rarely an issue before 1967. The Egyptians originally designated specific areas of unused government and *miri* land for the camps, though the middle camps were largely built on private land and these owners were offered comparable land in exchange, or the right to maintain ownership till UNRWA's mandate was terminated. The original shelters belonged to UNRWA, but all extensions have been built at the individual occupant's expense.

Whatever the legal status, the Israeli authorities now have

effective control. For the residents of the 30 shelters in Beach Camp bulldozed to rubble by the army in July 1983, UNRWA's lack of executive authority over the camps is starkly apparent. They have no means of appeal. Some of them have building permits issued by UNRWA before the Israeli occupation but these are no longer valid. If there are houses where the Israelis do not want them, then they will be removed.

Alongside this policy of thinning the camps, resettlement schemes began in 1975. There are eight housing projects in the Strip now twinning camps and projects (see Table 8.1). For example, Jabalia camp is to be absorbed by Beit Lahia and Jabalia Nazleh projects. Already, Beit Lahia project is encroaching on the camp and several houses are threatened with demolition to make way for it.

Haj Sheikh Radwan, at the northern edge of Beach Camp, has developed in three phases. It is one of three projects in Gaza Town. In 1976, after sewage, water and electricity had been brought to the area, 20 three-room houses were constructed. These model homes were shown off to journalists and refugees to raise interest in the project, but no more houses were built on this model. Instead, two-room houses built on 250m² plots were offered on 99-year leases. The registration fee was about $100, accepted on condition that the camp shelter should be destroyed within 12 months of the agreement. The contract is written in Hebrew, and few people know the conditions to their agreement or how the agreement could be revoked in the future. The houses were so shoddy that few survived the first winter, most leaked and some developed major faults which necessitated complete rebuilding. Those residents who had remittances from sons in the Gulf were able to rebuild their houses from scratch, others had to make do with patchy repairs and prepare as best they could for the next winter.

In 1978, the policy changed, and refugees were offered 125m² plots on which they could build their own homes. They received only $200 compensation for the demolished house in the camp and poured their life savings into building a new home. In 1982 the size of the plot was further reduced to 100m², and special priority was given to families living close to the sea. The coast has long been a security concern for the Israelis who intend to clear it of people the length of the Strip to make way for their 'Riviera' complex of hotels and restaurants.

Table 8.1
Government Housing Projects
(Information as at 31 December 1982)

Plots of Land

Area	Allo-cated pieces	Pieces under con-struction	Houses con-structed on pieces	Families	Persons	Pieces vacant
Jabalia, Beit Lahia	250	85	165	266	1590	—
Jabalia Nazleh	180	71	91	85	594	18
Gaza, Nasr	36	—	36	36	186	—
Gaza, Yarmouk	87	—	87	87	493	—
Gaza, Sheikh Radwan	611	325	257	299	1850	29
Khan Yunis, Al Amal	132	38	82	152	899	12
Rafah Brazil	107	18	82	128	803	7
Rafah Tal Es-Sultan	1500	110	311	352	2161	1079
	2903	*647*	*1111*	*1405*	*8576*	*1145*

Source: All the above figures have been obtained on the sites by UNRWA staff.

The houses are built in small blocks divided by two-lane streets, making army patrols easier. The Israelis no doubt also hope that having something to lose will stem refugee militancy. The projects fall within municipal boundaries though the services they receive are severely limited. The children may have more street to play in, but it is often just as squalid as in the camps. UNRWA has not been allowed to instal any of its services in the projects so refugees are increasingly dependent on the government. They are still eligible for UNRWA schools and clinics, but often their distance precludes their using them. Separating the refugees from UNRWA is one aspect of the general strategy of removing their refugee identity and breaking their connection with the past.

As the camps become noticeably thinner and the political implications more overt, popular committees have formed in the camps, mounting publicity campaigns to explain why the Israelis are trying to resettle the refugees. For most people it has been the acute problem of living space which has forced them to leave the camp. With no extensions to camp houses allowed, a two- or three-room shelter is no longer enough where one or two sons have married and started their own families in their parents' home. With space such an urgent need, it is hard to see what is humanitarian about the compulsory demolition of the camp shelters as a condition of moving to the project and with refugees' resistance to the resettlement projects growing it is unlikely that rehousing will be voluntary.

Notes

1. 'Palestine Refugees Today', *UNRWA Newsletter* No. 108, October 1984.
2. *Al Fajr* English, 2 December 1983.

9. Israeli Settlement in the Gaza Strip

The Labour Party's settlement policy in the Gaza Strip was markedly different from that which it followed in the Golan Heights, West Bank, Jerusalem suburbs and Northern Sinai. The Likud government inherited 105 settlements in 1977, of which only five were in the Gaza Strip. All of them were para-military forts without economic infrastructure or settled inhabit-ants. The Strip was considered too densely populated and of little historical or strategical importance, particularly while Israel controlled the Sinai. The policy of the Labour Party had been to surround the Strip with settlements just inside the Green Line and in Northern Sinai. Five *Nahals* (military outposts) were strategically placed down the backbone of the Strip, controlling the main road to Sinai and providing access to Gaza's precious water table. There were 20 settlements in Northern Sinai with about 4,500 settlers whose aim was to sever Gaza from Egypt, consolidating Gaza's isolation and facilitating control.

Likud's accession to power and the subsequent withdrawal from Sinai precipitated a marked change in settlement policy: a new drive for civilian settlement with advertisements aimed particularly at religious Jews extolling the beauties of Gaza's coast line. Blocks of settlements have been established whose economy is based on intensive hot-house agriculture and tourism. Their aim is to separate Palestinian population concentrations and create a Zionist presence in Gaza.

Each block is serviced by a new network of roads which avoid the Palestinian camps and towns. Schools, clinics, a theatre, banks, electricity and water supplies are completely separated from the indigenous population. This separation is so complete that one settler remarked that the only Arabs she saw were an occasional Bedouin on a camel in the distance. Some Sinai settlers were promised new housing in settlements in the Strip, particularly Mitzpe Atzmonah and Alai Sinai.

There are three major settlement blocks. The first, the northern block, consists of three settlements based around Nisanit which was built alongside the Erez industrial centre, set up in 1972 just across the Green Line. Nisanit was transformed from a military outpost to a civilian settlement in April 1982, three days after the Sinai withdrawal. The other two settlements in this cluster are Nevets Sala and Alai Sinai. They are both near the coast and as yet incomplete. They are planned to house 300 families each and to become recreational centres for religious Jews who would have direct access from Tel Aviv and Ashkelon to their as yet unspoiled beaches. In 1980, plans were drawn up to build an international airport in this area to supplement Ben Gurion airport, but this has not yet materialized.[1]

The second block is situated south of Gaza Town and consists of three settlements centred on Netzarim, which was established as a *Nahal* in 1972 and became a *Moshav* (village) in 1980 after land was expropriated from the Abu Mu'deen family. Alongside Netzarim there is a Kibbutz, also established in 1980. Both these settlements are situated in fertile land cultivated by Palestinians and their planned expansion would necessitate further expropriation. The third settlement in this block is Tel Montar which is still under construction. It is strategically placed overlooking Gaza Town and commands the Gaza-Rafah road as well as the main access road from the east to the settlements.

The third block is called Gush Qatif and contains eleven settlements, eight of which have been built by the Likud government. They have been constructed around Netzer Hatzani, one of the Labour-built settlements, and are all religious nationalist in orientation. The largest, Ganei Tal, has 242 inhabitants although it is planned that each should eventually house 120 families. Their economy is based on hot-house agriculture producing vegetables and flowers.

Outside these three major blocks there are two further settlements, both set up before 1977. Morag, in the south east of the Strip, has the elementary school which serves the Qatif block. Kfar Darom, which is the only settlement based on land which was owned by Jews prior to 1948, could be linked into the Qatif block because of its physical proximity and its religious orientation. It has a college for Torah studies supervised by the Ministry of Education.

During the election campaign of 1984, the construction of three more settlements was announced. One, called Yom Rafiah, sprang up in under four weeks next to the Egyptian border, complete with water, electricity and telephones. The other two are currently under construction.

Each of the settlements in the Gaza Strip, unlike those on the West Bank, is surrounded by barbed wire and guarded by soldiers. Most are built on sandy land with bungalow style houses, each with a small watered garden testifying to the agricultural potential of the Strip, given access to Gaza's water table. The settlers themselves are largely Ashkenazi and many of them are first-time settlers from America. 'As Jews we have an obligation to live here,' declared one from New York.[2] However, despite extensive advertising campaigns, generous loans and other incentives, Gaza's settlements lack settlers. Perhaps the most striking feature of these strange, isolated Swiss-village style colonies is that they seem empty. Air-conditioned mini-buses with tinted windows glide between them, but there are probably less than 1,000 settlers in the whole Strip.[3] The fierce and sustained military resistance to occupation between 1967 and 1971 earned Gaza a reputation among Israelis as something of a no-go area. Unlike many of the West Bank settlements, those in Gaza are too far from Israel's industrial centres to be a viable commuter base. The Israeli fear of Gaza, the uncompromising landscape and climate make Gaza a low priority for settlers, if not for the government. The Jewish Agency urged the government in 1982 to settle 100,000 Jews in the Strip, and their brochures describe the Gaza Strip as the Hawaii of Israel. But it is difficult to see how this could possibly be achieved. Those who do settle are either fervent religious nationalists or opportunists lured by the possibility of compensation in a future peace deal similar to the multi-million dollar handouts in the Sinai bonanza of 1982.

Notes

1. *Jerusalem Post*, 19 May 1980.
2. *Jerusalem Post*, 1 January 1979.
3. Meron Benvenisti, an Israeli researcher, estimated that there were 900 settlers in the Strip in 1983.
See also *Al Fajr* English Language Weekly, 1983.

Postscript to Chapter 9

Since we left the Strip, land confiscations have continued. With the existing settlements still ridiculously underpopulated, the continued expropriation of land becomes cynical to an unprecedented degree. The following is a translation of a report written by Dr Joseph al-Ghazi, secretary of the Israeli League for Civil and Human Rights, which appeared in the 15 February 1985 edition of *Al Fajr* English newspaper.

The occupation authorities in Gaza have begun to take steps to expropriate 5,000 *dunums* of agricultural land south of the city, near the Wadi Gaza bridge. Farmers were notified and 10 days ago grapevines were uprooted on one of the plots. In the middle of January 1985, a few dozen farmers in the Zaytun and Abu Midan blocs in Gaza, which respectively encompass 3,000 and 2,000 *dunums* of land, were ordered to appear before the deputy chief of the civil administration of Gaza, captain Adiv Hasson, on 21 January 1985. [Captain Hasson was involved in the incident in which Mohammed Hassan Abu Amra lost an eye, in May 1984.] Most of the land in question is being used for the cultivation of vineyards and orchards, some of which are up to 70 years old.

Upon arriving at the meeting, the farmers were sent to see Adiv Hasson one by one, and in the presence of officials from the Ministries of Finance and Agriculture and from the Israeli Land Authority, were told that their plots were state property and were ordered to leave them immediately; they were also told not to attempt to return to them, to stop cultivating their vineyards and orchards and to enter into negotiations with the compensation board set up by the civil administration. All of the farmers responded on the spot by saying that they would not allow their land to be expropriated and that they considered the authorities' attempt to be a case of sheer robbery. Furthermore, they said that they would continue to work their plots and would not accept compensation.

One of the farmers, Abd al-Karim Ism'il al-Taltini, whose family has been working 200 *dunums* of land in the Gaza Zaytun bloc together with a few other farmers since the Ottoman administration, told me that he spoke out against the expropriation in front of about ten other farmers, rejecting any attempt to negotiate compensation. Captain Adiv Hasson responded angrily by saying that the land would be expropriated by force if necessary. In order to lend credence to his statement, he sent a bulldozer and a bunch of soldiers to al-Taltini's fields on 23 January and they destroyed about 40 *dunums* of grapevines.

On 3 February, I visited the site. The terrain is sandy and there are many dunes there. I saw fruit trees and grapevines that are clearly decades old. Cultivating fruit trees and vineyards in this area demands a great deal of work over a long period of time; in order to overcome the effects of erosion, farmers plant saplings deep in the earth, sometimes five to six metres down, in order to exploit the layer of silt below the sandy surface. I saw the tracks of a bulldozer and scores of uprooted grapevines. It appears that the uprooting operations have been halted for the time being, in the wake of telegrams the farmers sent to the Red Cross representatives who visited the area a number of times.

I also visited Mohammed Zabut's plot, which was damaged two years ago when his grapevines and fruit trees were uprooted. When new vines began to sprout last year, they too were uprooted. I saw the remains of a house and well that had been destroyed by the authorities as well. Zabut was arrested after resisting the uprooting operations. He told me that 336 of his trees had been destroyed.

From the Gaza Zaytun bloc I could see the Netzarim settlement, the coast and the city of Gaza. The farmers repeatedly stressed the fact that they had worked the land without hindrance under Ottoman, British and Egyptian rule. They are not sure what the occupation authorities want to do with their land; is it being expropriated to make way for a new settlement or to expand Netzarim settlement? They believe that if the Zaytun and Abu Midan farmers are robbed of their land the farmers of Bir Saba' — south of Wadi Gaza and east of the railroad line — will be next.

10. Overview

Socially, Gaza remains considerably more conservative than the West Bank. The recent growth of Islamic fundamentalism, the maintenance of traditional arranged marriage procedures and a conservative attitude towards women are the result of a complex inter-relation of the pressures of occupation and the search for the preservation of the Palestinian identity. In the absence of a dynamic movement for political change, because of the repressive nature of the occupation, many Gazans seek to cling to traditions that have long since eroded in neighbouring countries and are anachronistic even in Gaza. This process has been accentuated by the impact of Israel's western-style society on Gaza. The majority of Gazans, certainly a majority of the men, have direct and regular contact with Israelis through labouring and trading. This creates a lot of pressure: Israeli society has certain superficially attractive features, such as more relaxed relations between men and women; but the majority of Gazans reject this comparative liberalism because it is seen as being Israeli: if the Israelis do it, it cannot be good. This can be seen, for example, in attitudes towards swimming in the sea: in Gaza, women do not swim unless fully clothed and then only rarely, so some families drive into Israel where there are no such restrictions. This has contributed towards an abnormal social growth in Gaza: because those Gazans who oppose the social traditions can get their release in Israel, the pressure for change within Gaza is dissipated.

A similar ambivalence exists within the context of shifting class and family loyalties. Class loyalties often conflict with national and family loyalties. The Gazan men and women and children who work in Israeli factories are exploited, unrepresented and in the eyes of their employers, dispensable as the demand and market fluctuate. Yet the national perspective of the Palestinians' struggle against Zionism precludes a class alliance with fellow Israeli workers at the factory or workplace. In addition, the perception by working-class Israelis of the Palestinians as a threat to their jobs works against such an alliance. Those Palestinians who work for Gazan capitalists, for example in the famous Seven Up bottling factory, are also exploited, unrepresented and dispensable. But the quest for a national liberation runs counter to organizing opposition based on class, even though the employer is an exploiter. The issue of class is subordinated to the need for a unified opposition to Zionism, but this very process limits the scope of that opposition.

The preservation of the power of the extended family is another constraint on the emergence of a class consciousness; yet it is the occupation which provides the need and rationale for maintaining and strengthening the family unit. Under such a powerful and all-pervasive assault as the occupation, it is the extended family which provides a measure of protection necessary for survival. It performs the functions that are gradually being assumed by the state in neighbouring countries: money for education and provision for the sick and elderly, for example. Perhaps more importantly in Gaza, the family provides the last line of defence, a layer of protection and support, against the occupation. It also presents a dilemma: the family provides necessary services, but also reinforces a hierarchical structure in society. Progressive groups and individuals are increasingly asserting that a prerequisite to tackling opposition is a substantial change in social attitudes, particularly with regard to the status of women. They maintain that unless this is achieved, any national solution would lead to the creation of a reactionary Palestinian state in which access to power for some groups — again, particularly women — would not be significantly improved. Yet it is the occupation itself which has provided the dynamic for the preservation of conservative attitudes.

Gaza's social composition reflects the traumas of its recent history. The refugee problem is still viewed with some hostility by the original population although this has been softened by an occupation which makes no such distinction. Eighty thousand people, about a sixth of the population, live in Gaza's twelve villages, and although they may be more conservative, their political aspirations do not differ significantly from those of people in the camps and towns.

There is a sizeable Bedouin community in the Strip who, having lost their land in 1948, moved to Gaza where many of them had traditionally spent their summers to avoid the heat and lack of vegetation in the Negev Desert. Many of them now live in shanty huts along the now disused railway line to Cairo and, robbed of their land, they too seek local agricultural work or labour in Israel. In some ways their situation is worse than that of the other refugees because many did not register with UNRWA in 1949 and so have no access to UNRWA facilities.

Coming into the Strip from the north, there is a roadblock manned by Israeli soldiers, and then a series of bold road signs in Hebrew indicating the distance to the Israeli settlement blocks. Settler traffic bypasses Gaza Town, avoiding the streets crowded with white Peugeot taxis, horses and donkeys pulling carts, street vendors selling *felafel*, *foul* beans and sweets, the women with their black dresses, white headscarves, often with shopping baskets on their heads: litter everywhere, men in cafés — the old with their *nargeelas* and the young looking and waiting, the Mercedes taxis plying the routes south and back and an oppressive, heavy heat which seems to reflect the atmosphere. But despite everything — the soldiers everywhere, the paralysis of initiative, the seemingly impossible odds of the struggle ahead, the divisions outside and their reflection inside, the prisons and the fear of the prisons, the paramount fear of every Gazan is expulsion. Thirty-seven years have not blunted the desire to return and to build again.